CH

For

MORMONS

And

JEHOVAH'S WITNESSES

CHECKMATE
For MORMONS
And JEHOVAH'S
WITNESSES

By

Dave Weeks

© 2013

Baptist World Cult Evangelism
P.O. Box 836
Dacula, GA 30019-0014
www.bwce.org

All quotations of Scripture are taken from the Authorized King James Version.

Additional citations are designated as follows:

NWT – *New World Translation*
JST – *Joseph Smith Translation*
BOM – *Book of Mormon*

CHECKMATE for MORMONS and JEHOVAH'S WITNESSES
© 2013 *Baptist World Cult Evangelism*
P.O. Box 836, Dacula, GA 30019-0014

Printed by Facing the Facts, Dacula, GA
Cover design by William McNeely, Jr.

Printed in the United States of America

All rights reserved. No part of this publication may be reproduced, stored in a retrieval system, or transmitted in any form or by any means, electronic, mechanical, photocopying, recording, or otherwise, without the prior written permission of the copyright holder.

Library of Congress Control Number: 2013951495

Weeks, Dave.
   Checkmate for Mormons and Jehovah's Witnesses / by Dave Weeks.
   p. cm.
   Includes bibliographical references and indexes.
   ISBN 978-0-9910115-0-6 (Paperback)
   ISBN 978-0-9910115-1-3 (Hardback)
   1. Church of Jesus Christ of Latter-Day Saints — Controversial literature. 2. Mormon Church — Controversial literature. 3. Jehovah's Witnesses — Controversial literature. 4. Witness bearing (Christianity). 5. Evangelistic work. I. Title.

FOREWORD

I have known David Weeks for many years, and it has been a privilege to have a part in the production of this his latest endeavor to reach souls for Christ. May the light of the glorious gospel of Christ so shine from these pages as to impart to its readers the knowledge of the glory of God in the face of Jesus Christ.

Richard Hughes
Richard Hughes Ministries, Inc.
P.O. Box 541, Cordele, GA 31010

ACKNOWLEDGMENTS

First of all, I would like to thank the Lord for my *help meet*, "Putter," my wife. She has been at my side for over 47 years. She is a very loving person, devoted to the Lord, serving Him in many ways. Her Facebook, Blog and "Putter's Pen" ministries are an encouragement to people in many different walks of life. May the sweet Lord give us the joy of serving Him until we hear the trumpet sounding.

A special thanks to Lois Harrison for helping with the first round of editing. She and her husband, Michael, have been great friends for many years. Lois has her Master's degree in Education and works as a curriculum developer.

Thanks to Richard Hughes, who helped with the final editing. We have been friends for many years. Brother Hughes taught English for 23 years at Tabernacle Baptist College in Greenville, South Carolina. He recently authored a book entitled, *An English Grammar for the Study of Scripture*.

Last, but not least, we thank Joanne Bowser of Calvary Baptist Church, York, PA. She did the last major proofread. Her work was meticulous. She demonstrated skills stemming from 30 years of experience. One of her degrees, which places her in the top rankings, is her degree of correctness.

DEDICATION

This writing is dedicated to my Saviour and Lord, Jesus Christ. May it be a blessing to all those who know the power of God's Word and who want to help others see their need of salvation, especially Mormon missionaries and Jehovah's Witnesses. One day they will be walking down your street and knocking on your door. When that day comes, you can be ready to speak with them, knowing what the Word of God can do in their hearts.

You need not feel defeated after a Mormon or a Jehovah's Witness has left your door. "May this book help you to become more effective in your dealings with those involved in these groups."

My prayer is this: "May the only true God, the One who is not willing that any should perish, enable these lost souls to see their need of salvation. May He give them no peace, nor rest, until they accept Jesus Christ, His Eternal Son, as their personal Lord and Saviour."

INTRODUCTION

Many times in the past thirty years I have spoken with Mormons and Jehovah's Witnesses (JWs), but I have never had the satisfaction of seeing them as bewildered and of knowing that they were sensing something wrong with what they have been told to believe as I have experienced in recent days. What is it that will cause a Mormon missionary or a JW to see the conflict between the Bible, God's Word, and what their leaders teach?

There are "tons" of books written on cults and how to evangelize them. If you are like me, reading those books proved of little or no help during an encounter with a cult member at your door. What you are about to read will provide the insight needed for a much better outcome in that situation.

Mormons and JWs always had something to say at the end of the conversation which allowed them to evade the reality that they are lost. It has been said many times that, unless a person realizes he is lost, there is no real sense of the need for salvation, regardless of how many Scriptures with which one is faced. Has that ever happened to you in your attempt to witness for the Lord? If so, then you know the pain of thinking you have failed – failed them and failed the Lord.

I have prayed a long time over this matter. Recently, the sweet Lord has given me the answers I have been seeking. I am writing this book to share with each of you the things the Lord has shown me. My heart's desire is to see all who are willing to experience, by the grace of God, the amazing power of God's Word working in the lives of Mormons and JWs succeed. Perhaps for the first time you will help them see their need of salvation.

If you want to sow seeds that will lead a soul to Christ somewhere down the road, then may the sweet Lord Jesus show you how to help Mormons and JWs see their need for salvation. May the blessed Holy Spirit work through us all!

TABLE OF CONTENTS

Chapter 1: What You Must Know — 1
    The Context Rule — 4
    The Harmony Rule — 5

Chapter 2: The Signs of the Time — 19
    The Signs of Christ — 20
    The Signs of the Apostles — 22
    The Signs of Satan — 23

Chapter 3: Mormon Checkmates — 29
    God's Concepts of Jesus — 34
    Cults' Concepts of Jesus — 36

Chapter 4: JW Checkmates — 41
    The Born-again Checkmate — 43
    The Resurrection Checkmate — 59
    The Michael Checkmate — 61
    The 144,000 Checkmate — 67
    The JW's Last Stand Checkmate — 75
    Jehovah is Jesus — 78

Chapter 5: The God Question — 83

Firstborn 85

First Created 85

Chapter 6: The Heaven Question 93

    What do Mormons teach? 94

    What do JWs teach? 101

    What does the Bible teach? 105

        God's Present Dwelling Place 106

        Present Home of the Redeemed 107

        The New Jerusalem 110

        The New Earth 110

Chapter 7: The Hell Question 117

    What do Mormons teach? 117

    What do JWs teach? 120

    What does the Bible teach? 124

Endnotes 137

Bibliography 141

Scripture Index 145

Subject Index 147

CHAPTER 1: What You Must Know

To be effective when witnessing to either Jehovah's Witnesses or Mormons, you must know this most important fact: you cannot tell them anything! If you begin a conversation by telling them something, it could create an atmosphere of contention. Kindness and compassion in your speech will give you a most welcomed introduction.

To be effective in your witness, you must learn to ask questions, questions that will cause them to see the conflicts between what they have been taught and the truth of God's Word. Your opinions will not matter; your emotions will not impress them. You must cause them to think, to see for themselves the conflict between God's truths and man's teachings.

Never read the Bible to them; rather, get them to read the Scriptures to you. Quoting the Bible to them, likewise, will not reach them. Make them read the Scriptures to you. This will cause them to focus on what they are seeing and hearing. This simple act of reading the Scriptures will give the Holy Spirit the opportunity to work in their hearts. He is the One who must (and can) reveal to them what is being said in the context of the Bible text.

This will take time. You must be prepared to spend that time. As they read the Scriptures out loud, then you can begin to ask them questions related to the Scriptures they are reading. However, there is one question with which you must begin. It is the first of a series of questions which will enable the Holy Spirit to bring them under conviction. The first question to ask is this: "Do you accept the Bible as your final authority for faith and life?"

The answer you are seeking is, "Yes." You must hear them clearly say that they accept the Bible as their final authority. They need to say publicly that they accept what the Bible teaches. This is the only common ground on which you and the one with whom you are dealing can successfully come together.

They will say, "Yes." Yet, at different times during the discussion, they will ignore what a verse of Scripture is clearly saying in favor of what their leaders have told them. When that happens (and as often as this happens), you must ask them again, "Is the Bible really your authority?"

When they say, "Yes," and affirm that it is so, then you can go on to the second question. The second question is this: "Are you now willing to take God at His Word?" By these two simple questions

("Do you accept the Bible as your final authority for faith and life?" and "Are you now willing to take God at His Word?"), you lay the groundwork for the Spirit of God to work in their hearts.

When you talk with either Mormons or JWs, you must understand that they believe God has chosen their prophet or their organization to be His propagator of truth to all the lost people in the world. They think of themselves as messengers of truth. They have no idea that they have been deceived and that they are lost.

What you must know is how, by the grace of God, to get Mormons and JWs to see that they are lost with absolutely no hope of salvation. That is your goal, to get them to see that they are without God and without hope. You cannot deviate from this end. If you do, you will have failed in your mission.

You cannot run rabbit trails; you cannot take short cuts or make detours. You must help them to see that they are lost. If you deviate, you will have missed the one God-given opportunity to see the Holy Spirit convict a soul that he is lost. Your goal is to "checkmate" their arguments after three moves.

Anyone who plays chess must learn and abide by the rules of play. Likewise, in witnessing to

Mormons or JWs, there must be some rules that they agree to follow or there is no chance for a checkmate. The Context and Harmony rules are two of the most important in rightly dividing the Word of Truth. They become the referees that govern the way a verse or passage of Scripture is to be understood. Without these rules, anything goes; with them, there is no wiggle room!

> 1. **Context Rule** – The applicable meaning of a word, phrase, sentence, or paragraph within a chapter or book of the Bible is taken from its circumstances and the conditions which surround it.

An example of the "Context Rule" is seen when dealing with the word *one* in John 10:28-30 –

> *And I give unto them eternal life; and they shall never perish, neither shall any man pluck them out of my hand.*
> *29 My Father, which gave them me, is greater than all; and no man is able to pluck them out of my Father's hand.*
> *30 I and my Father are one.*

Why did Jesus say that He and the Father are one? The word *hand* is the key, for there would be no difference if you were in the Father's hand or in Jesus' hand. There is no difference because both hands are divine. Some may say, "That is your interpretation." You may reply to them with this statement: "It is not a matter of interpretation; it is a matter of context." It is not what we are saying; it is what the Author is saying: what God is saying.

    2. **Harmony Rule** – A God-given truth will always be in harmony with the whole of God's Word.

An example of the "Harmony Rule" is found in Genesis 3:21 –

> *Unto Adam also and to his wife did the LORD God make coats of skins, and clothed them.*

Adam and Eve were saved by grace, repentance, and faith in the sacrifice that was offered. The animal garments represented the shedding of innocent blood and the death of the sacrifice. Those garments pictured what Christ would provide through the shedding of His blood and the laying down of His life in death at Calvary – that is *grace*. *Repentance* is represented by Adam and Eve's removing their garments (their own effort to take away their guilt and shame). *Faith* is represented by Adam and Eve's accepting God's sacrifice and putting on the garments of that sacrifice. No person has been, or ever will be, saved any differently.

Everyone who believes in God and who reads the Bible does not have the same understanding of what is being said. Why is that? Why do people come away from the Bible with a different understanding of the Bible? They differ in their understanding because not all people use the same rules to interpret what they read. There are rules of interpretation. When these rules are followed, they act as a referee who, without any bias, makes the same ruling in every like situation.

How important are the rules of interpretation? Extremely! Getting your subjects to agree to these rules at the beginning of your conversation is absolutely essential.

Next, you must know the moves Mormons and JWs will use to escape when you put them in check. Mormons will usually have three moves to avoid a checkmate. They will make the following claims:

1. "We have been told that not all Scripture has been translated properly."

2. "We believe one must have not only faith but also works in order to be saved."

3. "We have experienced the truth" as they give testimony to a feeling known as "the burning of the bosom."

The first one of their moves (where they declare, "We have been told that not all Scripture has been translated properly") is based on what they have been taught:

> *We believe the Bible to be the word of God as far as it is translated correctly; we also believe the Book of Mormon to be the word of God.*[1]

When someone says that the Word of God has been corrupted and that, therefore, God has inspired me to correct it, they are falling into a trick of the Devil. All attempts to undermine the authority of Scripture are simply re-enactments of what Satan did to Eve as recorded in Genesis.

Genesis 3:1-4 –
Now the serpent was more subtil than any beast of the field which the LORD God had made. And he said unto the woman, Yea, hath God said, Ye shall not eat of every tree of the garden?
2 And the woman said unto the serpent, We may eat of the fruit of the trees of the garden:

3 But of the fruit of the tree which is in the midst of the garden, God hath said, Ye shall not eat of it, neither shall ye touch it, lest ye die.
4 And the serpent said unto the woman, Ye shall not surely die.

Such attempts at undermining Scripture are also re-enactments of what Satan tried to do to Christ in the wilderness.

Matthew 4:1-10 –
Then was Jesus led up of the Spirit into the wilderness to be tempted of the devil.
2 And when he had fasted forty days and forty nights, he was afterward an hungred.
3 And when the tempter came to him, he said, If thou be the Son of God, command that these stones be made bread.
4 But he answered and said, It is written, Man shall not live by bread alone, but by every word that proceedeth out of the mouth of God.
5 Then the devil taketh him up into the holy city, and setteth him on a pinnacle of the temple,
6 And saith unto him, If thou be the Son of God, cast thyself down: for it is written, He shall give his angels charge concerning thee: and in their hands they shall bear thee

> up, lest at any time thou dash thy foot against a stone.
> 7 Jesus said unto him, It is written again, Thou shalt not tempt the Lord thy God.
> 8 Again, the devil taketh him up into an exceeding high mountain, and sheweth him all the kingdoms of the world, and the glory of them;
> 9 And saith unto him, All these things will I give thee, if thou wilt fall down and worship me.
> 10 Then saith Jesus unto him, Get thee hence, Satan: for it is written, Thou shalt worship the Lord thy God, and him only shalt thou serve.

Mormons will mention this first claim ("that not all Scripture has been translated properly") because they question the accuracy of the King James Version. The Mormon's first prophet, Joseph Smith, has made a revision of the King James, which leads them to their conclusion. Some of the explanations as to why Mormons question the accuracy of the Bible are readily available on the Internet.

The following are comments on this subject from Robert J. Matthews, who died in August of 2009. Mr. Matthews was "a Latter-day Saint religious educator and scholar, teaching in the departments of Ancient Scripture and Religious Education at Brigham Young University (BYU) in Provo, Utah."[2]

Joseph Smith, the first prophet of The Church of Jesus Christ of Latter-day Saints, made a "new translation" of the Bible, using the text of the King James Version (KJV). This work differs from the KJV in at least 3,410 verses and consists of additions, deletions, rearrangements, and other alterations that cause it to vary not only from the KJV but from other biblical texts. Changes range from minor details to fully reconstituted chapters. This article presents statements by Joseph Smith telling why he made a Bible translation, gives information relating to the development and production of the work, examines a number of the significant variants, and considers some doctrinal results and historical implications.[3]

AUTHORITY TO TRANSLATE.

The Prophet Joseph Smith claimed a divine appointment to make an inspired rendition or, as he termed it, a "new translation" of the Bible. This appointment can be illustrated by excerpts from his writings.

After laboring off and on for ten months on the early chapters of Genesis, Joseph Smith received a revelation from the Lord on March 7, 1831, directing him to begin work on the New Testament: "It shall not be given unto you to know any further concerning this chapter, until the New Testament be translated, and in it all these things shall be made known; wherefore I give unto you that ye may now translate it" D&C 45:60-61.[4]

PROCEDURE AND TIME FRAME.

When he began his work in 1830, Joseph Smith did not have a knowledge of biblical languages. His translation was not done in the usual manner of a scholar, but was a revelatory experience using only an English text. He did not leave a description of the translating process, but it appears that he would read from the KJV and dictate revisions to a scribe.[5]

Although written by Joseph Smith as a Bible translation, the Mormon Church only canonized two small sections of it: the book of Moses and part of Matthew chapters 23 and 24.

Since this work differs from the King James Bible, they view the KJV as an improper translation.

However, in his translation, John 1:3 did not come into question. Therefore, the checkmate is still in play.

Compare John 1:3, as found in the Joseph Smith "Translation" (JST), to John 1:3 in the King James Bible. You will notice that the combination of *any thing* to *anything* and an alternative relative pronoun were his only changes.

The first shows his changes to John 1:3 –

> *All things were made by him; and without him was not anything made which was made* (JST).

> *All things were made by him* [Jesus Christ]*; and without him was not any thing made that was made* (KJV).

In Joseph Smith's "translation," he changed the word *that* to the word *which*. He then combined the compound pronoun *any thing*, as previously mentioned. This has been a common practice since the 12th century.

The fact that the two verses are so close is very important because John 1:3 creates a conflict with the Mormon "Jesus." They assume that Christ was born after the universe was already in existence.

To the Mormon, God's creation is an organization of already existing matter.[6]

John 1:3 corrects this false assumption:

> *All things were made by him* [Jesus Christ]; *and without him was not any thing made that was made.*

Jesus Christ created the matter: "all things were made by him." There was no matter without him. There was nothing without him.

With these facts in mind, ask the Mormon who brings up this first objection: "Where is the evidence that John 1:3, or any other part of the King James Bible, is not translated correctly?"

If the Mormon claims that the Bible has been corrupted until the mid-1900s, when Mormon "prophets" corrected it, ask him, "Have you ever read John 1:3 in the JST?" (If you carry a smartphone, you can bookmark the web address www.lds.org/scriptures/jst/jst-john/1?lang=eng and let him read the verse for himself.)

If the King James Bible is false, then these words spoken by the Lord Jesus Christ would be false. But they are not false. They are true.

Matthew 5:18 –
For verily I say unto you, Till heaven and earth pass, one jot or one tittle shall in no wise pass from the law, till all be fulfilled.

Matthew 24:35 –
Heaven and earth shall pass away, but my words shall not pass away.

Their second move may be this declaration: "We believe one must have not only faith but also works in order to be saved." This move is a reference to the passages found in James, chapter 2.

James 2:14; 18-20; 26
14 What doth it profit, my brethren, though a man say he hath faith, and have not works? can faith save him?
18 Yea, a man may say, Thou hast faith, and I have works: shew me thy faith without thy works, and I will shew thee my faith by my works.
19 Thou believest that there is one God; thou doest well: the devils also believe, and tremble.
20 But wilt thou know, O vain man, that faith without works is dead?
26 For as the body without the spirit is dead, so faith without works is dead also.

With this move, they are attempting to put themselves in a good light because of their worldwide, door-to-door missionary work. The "check" of this move is to answer with the following truth: "Faith always works!" Then, you must follow with an explanation of that truth. I generally give them a couple of illustrations, using Muslims and JWs as examples.

Muslims, because of their faith, will strap a bomb to their bodies and walk into a crowded area and detonate it. JWs, because of their faith, will refuse a blood transfusion for themselves and their children, which many times results in unnecessary death. Yes, faith works; however, people cannot have faith in a false Jesus or a false God and have true salvation, no matter how good their works may be.

The third move to avoid checkmate may be the "bearing their testimony." This is the secret weapon of a Mormon; his testimony is his ultimate defense against all moves that would threaten him with a checkmate. The "burning of the bosom" is what the Mormons call their testimony. It is, to them, their personal confirmation from God Himself that the Book of Mormon is true.[7]

All Mormons put this supernatural, Satanic experience above any exposition of Scripture or any proof that one could offer to expose Joseph Smith or any of their prophets as false. They are told to read the Book of Mormon and, then, to pray and to ask God to verify that the Book of Mormon is true. As they are praying, they experience a burning in their chest. With this sign, they become believers in all of what Mormonism claims.

The only way that a Mormon will sense his need for true salvation is to have his testimony taken away from him. He must know that this sign (the burning in his chest often called the "burning of the bosom") did not come from God. You must take away from him his testimony. To do so, you might begin by asking the Mormon missionary if, in any of his door-knocking experiences, he has ever encountered a Pentecostal.

Most likely, he will say, "Yes." Then, you can ask the following: "Did you know that a Pentecostal believes that, because he has prayed and asked God for a sign (which is speaking in tongues), he has received his 'sign' from God? Do you believe that Pentecostals have the truth because they may have received the sign of tongues?"

The Mormon may not say anything in reply, but you can ask him another question: "Do you believe that the sign of tongues, which a Pentecostal may experience, comes from God?" Most likely, he will say, "No." Then you could ask him, "If Satan deceived him with a sign, would it be possible that he could deceive others also?"

He must understand that the only signs given in our day are the signs of Satan. You can use the material from the next chapter to show him the three different groups of signs taught in the New Testament: the signs of Christ, the signs of the apostles and the signs of Satan. The only signs given in our time are the signs of Satan.

Now that the Mormon no longer has his "testimony," you must assure him that he can trust the Bible, God's Word, as his only authority for faith and life. This is a good verse to ask him to read again:

> Matthew 24:35 –
> *Heaven and earth shall pass away, but my words shall not pass away.*

You may need to repeat the following statement often during your course of conversation: "You cannot believe in a false Jesus or a false God and have true salvation."

CHAPTER 2: The Signs of the Time

The signs of the time are here. People are eager to talk about what they have felt and seen. When you encounter someone who is trusting in a sign, ask them this question, "What makes your supernatural experience (or sign) any more authoritative than someone else's?" Signs are a deception.

Talk to a Pentecostal, and he will tell you that he knows he has the truth because of receiving the sign of tongues. This supernatural experience has convinced him that his faith is in the right place. Now that he has that "sign," he believes that Pentecostals are teaching the truth.

Talk to a Catholic who has been praying to one of the huge statues of Mary, especially if that statue has reportedly been either weeping or having blood drip from its hands, and she will tell you that she has the true religion. She is convinced that Mary does care for her soul. The "sign" has cemented this conviction in her heart. She knows the truth because of the sign.

Talk to a Mormon, and he will tell you the Book of Mormon is true because he prayed for a sign. Whether spiritual or physical, when he gets a feeling in his chest that is called the "burning of the bosom," he has found his answer. Now, you have a person who will put this sign above all other subjective truth, above speaking in tongues or seeing a statue bleed. You have a person who will place this sign within his chest above all objective truth, even the Word of God. No matter how much their "sign" may contradict the teachings of the Bible, it will become their assurance.

Have you sought for a sign? Have you trusted in a sign to know that you have the "truth"? From whom did your sign come?

The New Testament speaks of three different groups of signs. They are as follows:

1. The signs of Christ
2. The signs of the Apostles
3. The signs of Satan

The Signs of Christ

Toward the end of Christ's earthly ministry, he was asked for a sign. Both Pharisees and Sadducees had come to him. The Bible says that they were "tempting" Him, desiring He would show them a sign from heaven (Matthew 16:1). Notice how He responded to their seeking of a sign:

Matthew 16:4 –
A wicked and adulterous generation seeketh after a sign; and there shall no sign be given unto it, but the sign of the prophet Jonas.

Jesus Christ said that no sign would be given, except the sign of His resurrection.

Matthew 12:40 –
For as Jonas was three days and three nights in the whale's belly; so shall the Son of man be three days and three nights in the heart of the earth.

Jesus also taught His disciples that there would be a specific sign that would signal His second coming.

Matthew 24:30 –
And then shall appear the sign of the Son of man in heaven: and then shall all the tribes of the earth mourn, and they shall see the Son of man coming in the clouds of heaven with power and great glory.

These two signs are the only signs Christ said He would give. No other sign would be given. These are the only signs one can fully trust to be true, the only signs one can trust to be from God.

Revelation 1:7 –
Behold, he cometh with clouds; and every eye shall see him, and they also which pierced him: and all kindreds of the earth shall wail because of him. Even so, Amen.

The Signs of the Apostles

After the signs of Christ, the next grouping of signs is specific to the Age of the Apostles. We are speaking of the miracles performed by the Lord's apostles. The purpose of these signs was to validate the message of the gospel. The apostles raised the dead, cast out devils, made the lame to walk, healed the sick, etc. The Scriptures confirm that the signs of the apostles came from God:

Acts 5:12 –
And by the hands of the apostles were many signs and wonders wrought among the people....

2 Corinthians 12:12 –
Truly the signs of an apostle were wrought among you in all patience, in signs, and wonders, and mighty deeds.

The Signs of Satan

Since the time period in which the apostles lived,

there has been only one other group of active signs during the Church Age: they are the signs of Satan. Some examples of how Satan's signs convince people to follow a false religion are as follows:

1. Statues reportedly weeping tears

"In November of 2005, James Hattori, an NBC correspondent, reported on a statue of the Virgin Mary which appeared to be crying blood. About the Sacramento statue, Hattori reported, "It's either a pretty convincing hoax, some explainable physical phenomenon or, as some here believe, a miracle."[8]

2. People, after reading the Book of Mormon, getting a feeling in their chest of burning

"One of the foundations of Mormonism is its insistence that a person seek truth by praying for a private, special revelation from the Holy Spirit....What they receive is sometimes called a burning in the bosom as a confirmation of truth. Mormons frequently appeal to James 1:5 for this, especially given that their founder, Joseph Smith, claimed that this was the verse and method he used for finding the truth."[9]

"But, behold, I say unto you, that you must study it out in your mind; then you must ask me if it be right, and if it is right I will cause that your bosom shall burn within you; therefore, you shall feel that it is right."[10]

3. People experiencing unintelligible babbling (unknown tongues)

Reporting on the 53rd General Council of the Assemblies of God (AG), Orange County Convention Center, Orlando, Florida, Sept., 2009 –

"The South Texas AG District Council had sent a resolution – 'Reaffirmation of Pentecostal Distinctive: The Initial Physical Evidence of Holy Spirit Baptism' – to the council. The resolution noted that the Assemblies were formed on 'several biblical Pentecostal distinctives, not the least of which is the belief that the initial physical evidence of baptism in the Holy Spirit is speaking in other tongues.'

"It went on to say that in recent years, the practice 'has come under certain scrutiny.' The resolution called on the council to reaffirm the doctrine and 'continue to require our credentialed ministers to not only have the aforementioned Pentecostal experience in their own lives, but [to] actively preach and teach this doctrine as well."[11]

These supernatural, Satanic signs mislead people

into believing that they have the truth. Consider the following passages:

2 Thessalonians 2:9-12 –
Even him, whose coming is after the working of Satan with all power and signs and lying wonders,
10 And with all deceivableness of unrighteousness in them that perish; because they received not the love of the truth, that they might be saved.
11 And for this cause God shall send them strong delusion, that they should believe a lie:
12 That they all might be damned who believed not the truth, but had pleasure in unrighteousness.

2 Corinthians 11:13-15 –
For such are false, deceitful workers, transforming themselves into the apostles of Christ.
14 And no marvel; for Satan himself is transformed into an angel of light.
15 Therefore it is no great thing if his ministers also be transformed as the ministers of righteousness; whose end shall be according to their works.

Revelation 13:11-15 –

And I beheld another beast coming up out of the earth; and he had two horns like a lamb, and he spake as a dragon [the Devil].
12 And he exerciseth all the power of the first beast before him, and causeth the earth and them which dwell therein to worship the first beast, whose deadly wound was healed.
13 And he doeth great wonders, so that he maketh fire come down from heaven on the earth in the sight of men,
14 And deceiveth them that dwell on the earth by the means of those miracles which he had power to do in the sight of the beast; saying to them that dwell on the earth, that they should make an image to the beast, which had the wound by a sword, and did live.
15 And he had power to give life unto the image of the beast, that the image of the beast should both speak, and cause that as many as would not worship the image of the beast should be killed.

Revelation 16:14 –
For they are the spirits of devils, working miracles, which go forth unto the kings of the earth and of the whole world, to gather them to the battle of that great day of God Almighty.

Yes, it might truly be said that the "signs of the time" are the miracle signs of deception, used by Satan to deceive the lost. God's Word is not enough to most. Today, like in the days of Christ Himself, the unbelievers want more signs. However, the Bible alone is the only, and final, authority for all faith and truth.

The Bible will lead a seeking soul to the Saviour, giving him peace and confidence based on the promise of God's Word. A sign will lead a soul into Satan's snare. When that happens, the erring soul will say, "But, I felt it! I saw it! It must be true!"

Have Satan's signs and lying wonders become the source of your testimony?

CHAPTER 3: Mormon Checkmates

Learn how to ask questions that will cause people to see the conflict between what their leaders have taught them and what the Scripture says. By so doing, the Holy Spirit can use you to open their eyes and to convict them. One of the best examples that you can use, when dealing with a Mormon, is found in John 1:1-14 –

> *In the beginning was the Word, and the Word was with God, and the Word was God.*
> *2 The same was in the beginning with God.*
> *3 All things were made by him; and without him was not any thing made that was made.*
> *4 In him was life; and the life was the light of men.*
> *5 And the light shineth in darkness; and the darkness comprehended it not.*
> *6 There was a man sent from God, whose name was John.*
> *7 The same came for a witness, to bear witness of the Light, that all men through him might believe.*
> *8 He was not that Light, but was sent to bear witness of that Light.*
> *9 That was the true Light, which lighteth every man that cometh into the world.*
> *10 He was in the world, and the world was made by him, and the world knew him not.*

11 He came unto his own, and his own received him not.
12 But as many as received him, to them gave he power to become the sons of God, even to them that believe on his name:
13 Which were born, not of blood, nor of the will of the flesh, nor of the will of man, but of God.
14 And the Word was made flesh, and dwelt among us, (and we beheld his glory, the glory as of the only begotten of the Father,) full of grace and truth.

Begin by asking four questions, in this order:

1. Do you have a Bible with you?
2. Would you read John 1:1?
3. How do you know that John 1:1 is talking about Jesus?
4. Could you show me that from the context of the verses (John 1:1-14) you have just read?

When you ask them if they have a Bible, you can rest assured that they will have the KJV with them. They offer a copy to those whom they are visiting, using the Bible as a means by which to win men's trust.

After they have read the passage out loud, in response to your second question, you are in a position to ask the third question: "How do you know that John 1:1 is talking about Jesus?"

I addressed that question to one group of three Mormon missionaries who said to me: "Well, as Mormons, we believe it's talking about Jesus."

It is at this point that you can ask the fourth question, which will bring the Context Rule of interpretation into play: "Could you show me that from the context of the verses (John 1:1-14) you have just read?"

When I asked those same three Mormon missionaries that particular question, they went into a "huddle." After several minutes of reading verses and talking with one another, they turned toward me and said, "No!"

The reason they were having such a problem is that the Bible is not really their authority for faith and life. This is true with all cults and false religions. As Mormons, they are subject to the words of their "prophets," with the understanding that what the prophets say is the final authority for what Scripture says. They, like many others, have no concept of the authority the rules of context and harmony have in understanding what God is saying in His Word.

To show them how the rules of context and harmony explain the Scriptures and answer the question at hand (how we know that John 1:1 is speaking of Jesus), use a second set of questions based on John 1:14 –

And the Word was made flesh, and dwelt among us, (and we beheld his glory, the glory as of the only begotten of the Father,) full of grace and truth.

The three opening questions are as follows:

1. Would you read verse 14?
2. Does the verse not say that the Word was made flesh and dwelt among us?
3. Can we agree that, from the context, Jesus is identified as the "Word" who became flesh?

Take your time. Go from one step to the next, as they progress with you. Ask them to read verse 14. After they have read it, ask them for their acknowledgment of the Scripture: "Does the verse not say that the *Word* was made flesh and dwelt among us?" Allow them to answer, "Yes."

You have now demonstrated to them how that the context of the Scripture will explain itself. Now, it is time to focus on the Lord Jesus Christ from this passage, using the same rule of context. Turn their attention to John 1:1, and ask the following additional questions:

4. There is a verb in each of the three parts of this verse (John 1:1) that is exactly the same; could you tell me what that verb is?
5. Can you tell me what that verb means?

In asking the fourth question, I generally address it in this fashion: "Now, I have another question about John 1:1, with which, perhaps, you could help me. There is a verb in each of the three parts of this verse that is exactly the same; could you tell me what that verb is?"

They will be polite and be glad to help you regarding the verb used in each of the three parts of that verse. Once they tell you that the verb is the word "was," acknowledge their answer. I usually say, "Okay," and then proceed to the next question: "Can you tell me what that verb means?" They, most likely, will not have a clue.

You need to understand the three concepts found in John 1:1, in order to proceed any further. First, note the verse; then, note the concepts:

> *In the beginning was the Word, and the Word was with God, and the Word was God.*

God's Concepts of Jesus

1. The concept that Jesus is eternal: He has no beginning and no ending (John 1:1a).
2. The concept that Jesus is eternally with God: He is with the Father and with the Holy Spirit (John 1:1b).
3. The concept that Jesus is God: He is eternally a part of what God is (John 1:1c).

To understand John 1:1, we must know the meaning and use of the verb *was* in each of the three sentence parts in which it is employed in this verse. The word (*was*) is the past, singular form of the verb *to be*. The verb means *to exist*. All forms of the verb *to be* (*am, is, are, was, were, be, being, been*) function as a state of being (linking) or a helping verb.

Consider each of the three parts of this sentence:

1. *In the beginning was the Word,*
2. *And the Word was with God*
3. *And the Word was God.*

Part 1: *In the beginning was the Word*

This portion of the sentence answers the question:

"When did the Word exist?" The Word existed in a timeless past.

- Subject: *Word* (a title for Jesus)
- Verb: *was* (state of being, past tense)
- Complement: *in the beginning* (adverbial, time: existing in the past without a point of origin—eternally existing)

Part 2: *And the Word was with God*

This portion answers the question: "Where did the Word exist eternally?" The Word existed eternally with [the] God.

- Subject: *Word* (a title for Jesus)
- Verb: *was* (state of being, past tense)
- Complement: *with God* (adverbial, tells where He was eternally)

Part 3: *And the Word was God.*

This portion answers the question: "Who was the Word?" The Word was eternally God.

- Subject: *Word* (a title for Jesus)
- Verb: *was* (linking, past tense)
- Complement: *God* (predicate nominative, renaming the subject, *Word*)

What you have just done, in showing these truths methodically to the Mormons with whom you are dealing, is to reveal that their concept of Jesus represents a false Jesus. All of the cults present a false "Jesus" because all of the cults teach that Jesus had a beginning.

Having an understanding of John 1:1-3, by knowing the answers to the questions of *When*, *Where* and *Who* (as presented in verse 1), gives all Bible readers these Scriptural truths:

1. Jesus is eternal.
2. Jesus is the Creator of all things.

These truths will equip you to help those who have been misled by cult leaders. Mormons, JWs – and a number of other cults – they proclaim a false Jesus who is not eternal and not the Creator of all things. Consider some examples of what cult leaders are teaching their followers.

Cults' Concepts of Jesus

The Watchtower "Jesus" – He is God's First Created Being, which means he had a beginning.

> *Jesus is Jehovah's most precious Son—and for good reason. He is called "the firstborn of all creation," for he was God's first*

creation.¹²

The Mormon "Jesus" – He is the First Spirit Child of Elohim, which means he had a beginning.

> *Every person who was ever born on earth was our spirit brother or sister in heaven. The first spirit born to our heavenly parents was Jesus Christ,¹³ so he is literally our elder brother.¹⁴*

The Adventist "Jesus" – He is Michael, the Archangel, which means he had a beginning.

> *When Jesus stands up: when his work is finished in the Most Holy, then there will be not another ray of light to be imparted to the sinner...The light is made to reach far ahead, where all is total darkness. MICHAEL stands up.¹⁵*

The Moslem "Jesus" – He is just a prophet and only a man, which means he had a beginning.

> *Surely the likeness of Isa [Jesus] is with Allah as the likeness of Adam; He created him from dust, then said to him, Be, and he was (The Quran, Surah 3:59).*

In contrast to the cults, the Bible declares two great

truths regarding Jesus.

1. Jesus is eternal.
2. Jesus created all things.

The Jesus of the Bible is eternal: He has no beginning and no ending. The following verses declare that Jesus existed in the beginning, without any point of origin. They are an explicit reference to Christ's eternality:

> John 1:1a –
> *In the beginning was the Word...*

Notice the words *in the beginning* and *the Word was* (being in eternity past).

> Hebrews 7:3 –
> *Without father, without mother, without descent, having neither beginning of days, nor end of life; but made like unto the Son of God; abideth a priest continually.*

Notice the words *...having neither beginning of days, nor end of life....* Christ's eternality is clearly presented by such wording.

The Jesus of the Bible created all things. The fact that Jesus created all things is the proof that He was not a created being.

John 1:3 –
All things were made by him; and without him was not any thing made that was made.

Colossians 1:15, 16 –
Who is the image of the invisible God, the firstborn of every creature:
16 For by him were all things created, that are in heaven, and that are in earth, visible and invisible, whether they be thrones, or dominions, or principalities, or powers: all things were created by him, and for him:

To understand the figurative use of the term "firstborn," note Psalm 89:27 –

Also I [Jehovah speaking] *will make him* [David] *my firstborn, higher than the kings of the earth.*

Leaving John 1:1-3 and going to Colossians and Psalms is most often too time-consuming. You run the risk of presenting too much detail. If they are presented with too much detail, they will lose interest and leave.

All that a Mormon needs to see in order for him to understand he is lost is that the Mormon "Jesus" is not eternal, nor the Creator of all things. Therefore, his "Jesus" is a false Jesus. One cannot believe in a false Jesus and a false God and have true salvation.

Do not lose too much time talking at this point. Make the move to "checkmate" by using these words: "How could you possibly have any hope by believing in a false god?"

Ask the Mormon to read John 1:3, once again, and then say, "If you only believed this one verse in the Bible, you could never honestly be a Mormon."

The three Mormon missionaries who heard these things spoken to them left with no response other than the look of Holy Spirit conviction on their faces. Checkmate! The Word will continue to work!

CHAPTER 4: JW Checkmates

To introduce JW checkmates, you need to know the three main theological differences to which JWs subscribe:

1. They deny the Trinity.
2. They deny immortality.
3. They deny eternal punishment.

These are not the only false teachings of the Jehovah Witness; but, among their many false teachings, these three are the ones with which JWs seem most often challenged when going door to door. Among their false teachings is, perhaps, the most brainwashing message of the Watchtower (WT) organization. This false teaching declares that, in 1919, JWs fulfilled prophecies in Scripture concerning Israel's restoration. In so doing, they became the "spiritual Nation of Israel" of the last days.[16]

Watchtower leaders give to themselves the authority of being the "anointed ones." They declare that they are the 144,000 mentioned in Revelation 7 and in Revelation 14. It is to them God has given His kingdom authority. They believe that He instructs them and that they carry out His will.[17]

This claim is the weakest link in their theological chain of errors. It is a very easy claim to counter if one knows the chronology of events in Matthew 24 and the three divisions of the Book of Revelation. Learn these checkmates, and you will see JWs fatally wounded, with no chance of recovery.

The most important concept for people to understand is this concept: to know who Jesus is. Their nationality makes no difference; their background grants no grace – all people need to know who Jesus is. One cannot believe in a false Jesus and have true salvation. It is only by the grace of God that the blind can see.

Recall what is meant by a "checkmate." When you witness to anyone and he leaves knowing that he is lost, you have achieved a checkmate. Their knowledge that they are lost is the checkmate. Their "game" is over; they have no more excuses, no more wiggle-room. When a man has no way to escape, knowing that he is lost without any hope, he has a chance to listen to God and to find forgiveness and salvation in Jesus Christ.

There are five checkmates for JWs. Those checkmates are as follows:

   1. The Born-again Checkmate
   2. The Resurrection Checkmate

3. The Michael Checkmate
4. The 144,000 Checkmate
5. The JW's Last Stand Checkmate

The first of these checkmates is the most difficult for a JW because it causes him the most concern. I call this the "Born-again" Checkmate. Jesus said it to Nicodemus: "Ye must be born again" (John 3:7).

The BORN-AGAIN Checkmate

The Watchtower teaches their followers that only 144,000 people may enter the kingdom of heaven (Revelation 7 & 14), that only the 144,000 have the possibility of being born-again. Consider this example, taken from a Watchtower article, dated April 1st, 2009, entitled: "The New Birth – What Is Its Purpose?"

> *Many believe that one needs to be born again to receive eternal salvation. Note, though, what Jesus himself said about the purpose of the new birth. He stated: "Unless anyone is born again, he cannot see the kingdom of God." (John 3:3) Thus, one needs to be born again in order to enter into God's Kingdom, not in order to receive salvation. 'But,' some may say, 'are not these two expressions—entering the*

Kingdom and receiving salvation—referring to the same reward?' No, they are not. To understand the difference, let us consider first the meaning of the expression "kingdom of God."

A kingdom is a form of government. So, then, the expression "kingdom of God" means "government of God." The Bible teaches that Jesus Christ, the "son of man," is the King of God's Kingdom and that Christ has fellow rulers. (Daniel 7:1, 13, 14; Matthew 26:63, 64) Furthermore, a vision given to the apostle John disclosed that Christ's fellow rulers are individuals chosen "out of every tribe and tongue and people and nation" and will "rule as kings over the earth." (Revelation 5:9, 10; 20:6) God's Word further reveals that those who will rule as kings form a "little flock" of 144,000 individuals "who have been bought from the earth."—Luke 12:32; Revelation 14:1, 3.[18]

To the contrary, being born-again is equated in Scripture with receiving eternal salvation. This truth can be shown from *the New World Translation* (NWT).

Luke 18:18-30 (NWT) –
And a certain ruler questioned him, saying:

"Good Teacher, by doing what shall I inherit everlasting life?" 19 Jesus said to him: "Why do you call me good? Nobody is good, except one, God. 20 You know the commandments, 'Do not commit adultery, Do not murder, Do not steal, Do not bear false witness, Honor your father and mother.'" 21 Then he said: "All these I have kept from youth on."
22 After hearing that, Jesus said to him: "There is yet one thing lacking about you: Sell all the things you have and distribute to poor people, and you will have treasure in the heavens; and come be my follower." 23 When he heard this, he became deeply grieved, for he was very rich. 24 Jesus looked at him and said: "How difficult a thing it will be for those having money to make their way into the kingdom of God! 25 It is easier, in fact, for a camel to get through the eye of a sewing needle than for a rich man to get into the kingdom of God." 26 Those who heard this said: "Who possibly can be saved?" 27 He said: "The things impossible with men are possible with God." 28 But Peter said: "Look! We have left our own things and followed you." 29 He said to them: "Truly I say to you, There is no one who has left house or wife or brothers or parents or children for the sake

of the kingdom of God 30 Who will not in any way get many times more in this period of time, and in the coming system of things everlasting life."

Notice the following:

- "By doing what shall I inherit everlasting life (v. 18)?"
- "…treasure in the heavens" (v. 23).
- "…make their way into the kingdom of God (v. 24)!"
- "…the kingdom of God" (v. 25).
- "…for the sake of the kingdom of God" (v. 29).
- "…everlasting life" (v. 30).

What the Watchtower ignores completely is the fact that, from the beginning of creation, the kingdom of God has existed in two places. The Kingdom of God existed in heaven, where God created the angels and gave them kingdom authority; and, it existed on earth, where He created man and gave him earthly kingdom authority. God was present with man daily in the garden.

Consider Genesis 1:1 and Genesis 1:26-28 as shown in the New World Translation (NWT).

Genesis 1:1 (NWT) –
In [the] beginning God created the heaven and the earth.

Genesis 1:26-28 (NWT) –
And God went on to say: "Let us make man in our image, according to our likeness, and let them have in subjection the fish of the sea and the flying creatures of the heavens and the domestic animals and all the earth and every moving animal that is moving upon the earth." 27 And God proceeded to create the man in his image, in God's image he created him; male and female he created them. 28 Further, God blessed them and God said to them: "Be fruitful and become many and fill the earth and subdue it, and have in subjection the fish of the sea and the flying creatures of the heavens and every living creature that is moving upon the earth."

Matthew 21:43 –
Therefore say I unto you, The kingdom of God shall be taken from you, and given to a nation bringing forth the fruits thereof.

These verses prove that the kingdom of God also exists on earth.

To be born-again means being "born from above" or "born of God." We become a child of God through a spiritual birth which takes place as stated in John 1:12-13 (NWT) –

> However, **as many** as did receive him, to them he gave authority to become **God's children**, because they were exercising faith in his name; 13 and **they were born**, not from blood or from a fleshly will or from man's will, but **from God**.

There are, in reality, only two groups of people in the world: the children of God and those who are not the children of God. If one is not born-again, he will never see nor enter into God's Kingdom, whether on earth or in heaven.

Notice, also, that John 1:12, says, *as many*. The expression *as many* has no limits. The basis of becoming a child of God is faith in Jesus, as shown in John 1:1-3 (NWT) –

> In [the] beginning the Word was, and the Word was with God, and the Word was a god. 2 This one was in [the] beginning with God. 3 All things came into existence through him, and **apart from him not even one thing came into existence** what has come into existence.

One cannot believe in a false Jesus (that is, any Jesus who is not eternal and not the Creator of all things) and have true salvation. The Watchtower teaches that Jesus is Michael the archangel, God's first created being.[19] If such a thing were true, then Jesus could not have created all things.

Setting up this checkmate requires a few moves of agreement. Here is a list of the questions we will be discussing:

1. "Do you believe that from the beginning of creation the kingdom of God always existed in two places: in heaven where God created the angels and on earth where He created man?"

2. "Would you also agree that in reality there are only two classes or groups of people in all the world: the righteous and the unrighteous, or the righteous and the wicked, or the godly and the ungodly, or the sheep and the goats, or the wheat and the tares, or the saved and the unsaved, or the children of God and the children of the Devil?"

3. "How does one become righteous?" (And, if the JW does not have the right answer to this

question, ask, "To which group would you belong?").

4. "So, how do the Scriptures tell us that someone becomes *righteous, saved* or, in other words, becomes *a child of God*?"

5. "How could you, as a JW, have any hope of seeing or entering God's kingdom on earth, if you have never been born-again (had a spiritual birth); for, the Watchtower teaches that only the 144,000 can be born-again?"

The first question you must have the JW agree with is as follows: "Do you believe that, from the beginning of creation, the kingdom of God always existed in two places: in heaven, where God created the angels, and on earth, where he created man?" Remember, to a JW, *kingdom* means a form of government where there is a ruler and subjects. In heaven, God would be the ruler and the angels the subjects. On earth, God would be the ruler and man, along with all creation, would be His subjects.

In each of these kingdoms, there are rank and file, and dominion. Lucifer was the highest order of the heavenly creatures; on earth, Adam had been given dominion to rule the earth. This is new information to a JW, and it might be puzzling to him. He has been told that there is only one kingdom and that the one kingdom is heaven. You need to be ready to ask him to read two verses, Genesis 1:1 and 1:26, so that he can make the connection himself and see that two kingdoms do exist.

>Genesis 1:1 –
>*In the beginning God created the heaven and the earth.*

>Genesis 1:26 –
>*And God said, Let us make man in our image, after our likeness: and let them have dominion over the fish of the sea, and over the fowl of the air, and over the cattle, and over all the earth, and over every creeping thing that creepeth upon the earth.*

You must get agreement on this point in order to create the checkmate move when you get to John 3:3 and 3:7. However, there are several additional points that must first be established.

Once you have shown the JW that there are two kingdoms, ask him to read Psalm 37:29 from the Watchtower's Bible (NWT).

>Psalm 37:29 –
>*The righteous themselves will possess the*

earth, And they will reside forever upon it.

Then ask this question: "Would you also agree that, in reality, there are only two classes or groups of people in all the world: the righteous and the unrighteous, or the righteous and the wicked, or the godly and the ungodly, or the sheep and the goats, or the wheat and the tares, or the saved and the unsaved, or the children of God and the children of the Devil?"

Once you have gone through this extensive list, they will, without hesitation, agree. What you would want to keep back until after you have dealt with John 3:3-7, is where the righteous will spend eternity – the answer to which is, "On the earth." They do not know that, and you may wish to respond to their surprise in the following manner:

> "What! You mean you did not know that?"

> "Why are you so shocked? Psalm 37 is just one of many places in Scripture where this truth is mentioned."

Stay on the path of "the righteous." Since the JW has agreed that there are only two groups of people in the world (the righteous and the unrighteous or the children of God and those who are not the children of God), ask him the question, "How does one become righteous?"

If the JW does not have the right answer to this question, ask him, "To which group would you belong, the righteous or the unrighteous?"

Most likely, the JW will say this: "He that endures until the end will be saved." This statement is taken from Matthew 24:13 –

> *But he that shall endure unto the end, the same shall be saved.*

Regardless of his answer, you want him to see what the Bible declares about the righteous. Ask him to read these verses from Romans:

> Romans 4:1-5 –
> *What shall we say then that Abraham our father, as pertaining to the flesh, hath found?*
> *2 For if Abraham were justified by works, he hath whereof to glory; but not before God.*
> *3 For what saith the scripture? Abraham believed God, and it was counted unto him for righteousness.*
> *4 Now to him that worketh is the reward not reckoned of grace, but of debt.*
> *5 But to him that worketh not, but believeth on him that justifieth the ungodly, his faith is*

counted for righteousness.

Note the following about this passage:

> *Abraham believed God and it was counted unto him for righteousness.*

Ask this question: "So, how do the Scriptures tell us that someone becomes *righteous, saved,* or, in other words, becomes *a child of God*?"

Then, ask the JW to read Romans 4:1-5 again. When he finishes reading, he will most likely make a reference to James 2. If he does, make sure he reads these verses also, for they repeat the Romans passage by declaring that Abraham was justified by faith:

> James 2:21-23 –
> *Was not Abraham our father justified by works, when he had offered Isaac his son upon the altar?*
> *22 Seest thou how faith wrought with his works, and by works was faith made perfect?*
> *23 And the scripture was fulfilled which saith, Abraham believed God, and it was imputed unto him for righteousness: and he was called the Friend of God.*

Does James 2 contradict both itself and Romans 4 when it states that Abraham was justified by works? The answer is, "No!" Righteousness is not achieved; it is received or imputed by God through faith.

When Abraham believed God, his faith and works increased together. True faith always works, and it always glorifies God. The works of a false faith will end in death and destruction, for one cannot believe in a false god or a false Jesus and have true salvation.

Abraham's righteousness was not justified by his works but by his faith. Abraham's faith was justified by his works, meaning his works vindicated that his faith was genuine. It was proven by his obedience.

Faith justifies a man before God; works justify a person before men. James 2 is simply a rebuke to those who claim to be saved, while being continuously disobedient to God's Word. First John 2:4 makes this clear:

> *He that saith, I know him* [Christ], *and keepeth not his commandments, is a liar, and the truth is not in him.*

When the JW sees (and indicates so by some means of acknowledgment, such as a nod of the head) that a man is made righteous by faith and not by works, then ask him to read the following passage:

> John 3:3-7 –
> *Jesus answered and said unto him, Verily, verily, I say unto thee, Except a man be born again* [have a spiritual birth], *he cannot see the kingdom of God.*
> *4 Nicodemus saith unto him, How can a man be born when he is old? can he enter the second time into his mother's womb, and be born?*
> *5 Jesus answered, Verily, verily, I say unto thee, Except a man be born of water and of the Spirit, he cannot enter into the kingdom of God.*
> *6 That which is born of the flesh is flesh; and that which is born of the Spirit is spirit.*
> *7 Marvel not that I said unto thee, Ye must be born again* [spiritual birth].

Now, for the checkmate question: "How could you, as a JW, have any hope of seeing or entering God's kingdom on earth, if you have never been born-again (had a spiritual birth), for the Watchtower teaches that only the 144,000 can be born-again?"

They may say: "There are many different opinions of what it means to be born-again."

To this you should reply, "Yes, that is true, John 3 tells a person he must be born-again; but, John 1:12-13 tells a person how he must be born-again."

Ask them to read John 1:12-13 –

> *But as many as received him* [Jesus Christ], *to them gave he power to become the sons of God* [born-again from above or a spiritual birth, become a child of God], *even to them that believe on his name:*
> *13 Which were born, not of blood, nor of the will of the flesh, nor of the will of man, but of God.*

Note the three negative statements:

1. Not of blood
2. Nor of the will of the flesh
3. Nor of the will of man

These three phrases tell one how he cannot be born of God. First, not through one's blood-line: being born into a Christian family would not make one a child of God. Second, not of one's "self": a person, by himself, cannot just decide to become a Christian by some act of his flesh or of his own will. Third, not by the will of man: no man can, by laying hands on a person or sprinkling him with water, make that person a child of God.

How, then, can a man be born-again? He can be born-again when he is born of God. When a person believes in John 1:1-3 and receives by faith this Jesus who is eternal and the Creator of all things, he will have a spiritual birth and become a child of God.

Look the JW in his face and, with great compassion, ask him, "How could you have any hope if you do not know how to become righteous, and if you do not believe that Jesus is eternal and the Creator of all things, and that not even one thing was created that He did not create? If you have never truly been born-again, how could you have any hope?"

Before leaving this section, recall that I asked you to "keep back" some information on where the righteous will spend eternity (p. 52). It is a surprise to JWs to be told that eternity will be spent on the earth.

A second and much shorter way to create the born-again checkmate is to ask the question: "Who are the righteous?" The following two Scriptures make it clear that the "righteous" are those who are born-again.

> 1 John 3:9-10 –
> *Whosoever is born of God doth not commit*

sin; for his seed remaineth in him: and he cannot sin, because he is born of God.
*10 In this the **children of God** are manifest, and the **children of the devil**: whosoever doeth not righteousness is not of God, neither he that loveth not his brother.*

1 John 2:29 –
*If ye know that he is **righteous**, ye know that every one that doeth righteousness is **born of him**.*

The RESURRECTION Checkmate

The bodily resurrection of Jesus Christ is one of the essential doctrines that a person must believe when receiving Christ as his or her personal Saviour. The Watchtower teaches that the crucified body of Jesus was destroyed and that He was recreated as a "spirit-being." Unbeknownst to JWs, what they really believe is called "reincarnation."

The following is a quote from an article entitled, "The Fleshly Body of Jesus," Watchtower, 1953, September 1st. The article explains what they teach concerning the body of our crucified Lord and risen Saviour.

JESUS' FLESHLY BODY DISSOLVED

Jesus was the antitype foreshadowed by Moses, the great mediator and leader of the congregation of Israel. God himself disposed of Moses' body by burial, and "no man knoweth of his sepulchre". (Deut. 34:5, 6) Later, one of the Christian writers says that Michael had a dispute with the Devil over the body of Moses. (Jude 9) The Devil desired to get the body of Moses the great leader and to use it as an object of worship to draw the Israelites away from their true invisible Commander and Leader, Jehovah God. With stronger desire the Devil wanted to obtain the fleshly body of Jesus after his death to induce some to worship it and use it for indecent false religious purposes, thus reproaching Jehovah God. But Jehovah thwarted the Devil's purpose in both cases by disposing of the bodies of these two faithful men.

Moses' body returned to the dust by process of decay, as all human bodies do, but not so in Jesus' case, for it is written: "For thou wilt not leave my soul to Sheol; neither wilt thou suffer thy holy one to see corruption." (Ps. 16:10, AS; Acts 2:31) So God caused Jesus' body to disappear, but not corrupt, meaning that it was dissolved, disintegrated back into the elements from which all human bodies are made.[20]

Facing the Facts (a small printing ministry of Baptist World Cult Evangelism) has in print a 4x6 card with the above quote on the front and, on the back, a definition of the terms *reincarnation* and *resurrection*, along with the verses in Scripture that capture the truth of Christ's bodily resurrection. The card is free, and available by request. When the card is folded, it fits neatly into a shirt pocket. It will make you "armed and dangerous." Whenever the next JW approaches you unexpectedly, you will be ready to make a move that could lead to a checkmate.

The MICHAEL Checkmate

Charles Taze Russell was the first Watchtower leader. Since the days of his affiliation with the Seventh-Day Adventists, he and all other Watchtower governing body leaders (the 8-12 men that head the WT organization) have taught that Jesus Christ is Michael the archangel. The maze which leads to this conclusion is puzzling to average JWs, but they are required to accept the Watchtower's teachings without question.

To doubt any Watchtower explanation of Scripture is considered an act of rebellion against Jehovah and his organization. That rebellion, if continued, will lead to one's "disfellowshipping," which means the loss of salvation. One example of the Watchtower's twisted versions of Jesus being Michael, taken from Watchtower 1979, February 15th, "Questions from Readers":

> *After his resurrection Jesus Christ, whom we understand from the Scriptures to be Michael the archangel, was to 'sit at God's right hand' until it was time for him to "go subduing in the midst of [his] enemies.*[21]

Ask the JW if the Watchtower teaches that Jesus Christ is Michael the archangel. When he replies, "Yes," ask him to show you a Scripture that says Michael, the archangel, is Jesus. There are five direct references to Michael in Scripture. None of them, in their context, says that Jesus is Michael. You should have this list memorized and know which one of the five is the most damaging to the Watchtower's claim.

The five direct references to Michael are as follows: Daniel 10:13; Daniel 10:21; Daniel 12:1; Jude 1:9; and Revelation 12:7.

Daniel 10:13 –
But the prince of the kingdom of Persia withstood me one and twenty days: but, lo, Michael, one of the chief princes [implying

there is more than one], *came to help me; and I remained there with the kings of Persia.*

Daniel 10:21 –
But I will shew thee that which is noted in the scripture of truth: and there is none that holdeth with me in these things, but Michael your prince.

Daniel 12:1 –
And at that time shall Michael stand up, the great prince which standeth for the children of thy people: and there shall be a time of trouble, such as never was since there was a nation even to that same time: and at that time thy people shall be delivered, every one that shall be found written in the book.

Jude 1:9 –
Yet Michael the archangel, when contending with the devil he disputed about the body of Moses, durst not bring against him a railing accusation, but said, The Lord rebuke thee.

Revelation 12:7 –
And there was war in heaven: Michael and his angels fought against the dragon; and the dragon fought and his angels.

Notice that Daniel 10:13 calls Michael "one of the chief princes." Also, in Jude 1:9, there is a distinction made between Michael and the Lord.

The key verse that makes the Watchtower's claim impossible is Daniel 10:13. This verse clearly states that Michael is just "one of the chief princes," implying that there are more "chief princes," even though they are not mentioned by name. This means Michael is not unique and could not be the only begotten of the Father.

The point that Scripture makes is that Jesus Christ is far above every government and every authority, whether on earth or in heaven. He is King of kings and Lord of lords. Michael dared not rebuke the Devil, as stated in Jude 9, but Jesus did (and does) have the power to rebuke him.

> Revelation 17:14 –
> *These shall make war with the Lamb, and the Lamb shall overcome them: for he is Lord of lords, and King of kings: and they that are with him are called, and chosen, and faithful.*

> Philippians 2:10, 11 –
> *That at the name of Jesus every knee should bow, of things in heaven, and things in earth, and things under the earth;*

> *11 And that every tongue should confess that Jesus Christ is Lord, to the glory of God the Father.*

> Matthew 4:10 –
> *Then saith Jesus unto him, Get thee hence, Satan: for it is written, Thou shalt worship the Lord thy God, and him only shalt thou serve.*

Although these five passages are the only mentions of Michael in Scripture, the Watchtower endeavors to prove that Jesus is Michael the archangel by placing a spin on 1 Thessalonians 4:16. The following quote is from a Watchtower article entitled, "Do You Remember?" It comes from the April 15th issue, 1991:

> *Why do we conclude that Jesus is the archangel Michael? God's Word mentions only one archangel, and it speaks of that angel in reference to the resurrected Lord Jesus: "The Lord himself will descend from heaven with a commanding call, with an archangel's voice and with God's trumpet." (NWT 1 Thessalonians 4:16) At Jude 9 we find that this archangel's name is Michael.*[22]

The first part of their argument for Jesus being Michael the Archangel is inconclusive and speculative. Although archangels are only mentioned twice in Scripture, and only once by name, this does not mean that there could not be more that are unnamed. Daniel 10:13, in the NWT, states that Michael is just "one of the foremost princes," meaning there are more who are obviously unnamed.

The second part of the Watchtower's argument is based on a misunderstanding of what is stated in the passage found in 1 Thessalonians 4:16 –

> *For the Lord himself shall descend from heaven with a shout, with the voice of the archangel, and with the trump of God: and the dead in Christ shall rise first.*

The statements *with an archangel's voice* and *the trump of God* are simply saying that the archangel, like God's trumpet, will herald the coming of the Lord Jesus Christ. It is not saying that Jesus is Michael the archangel. The statement in Jude 9, which declares that Michael is an archangel, cannot be linked in context or in anyway hermeneutically to 1 Thessalonians 4:16 in order to make it appear that Jesus and Michael are the same person.

The 144,000 Checkmate

JWs are taught that the numbering of the 144,000 anointed Christians began with the Lord's disciples and continued into the Church Age. All of the members of the Watchtower's governing body (those who run the organization in Brooklyn) claim to be anointed and among the 144,000. There is a great deal more that could be said about this subject, but this is all that one needs to know in order to execute the checkmate.

> *So, during that long period of more than 1,900 years since Christ's ascension to heaven, God has been very selective. He has not been trying to save the world. The saving of all mankind who will obediently give response to God's commands will be accomplished during Christ's thousand-year reign over earth. During the past 1,900-year period God has been selecting those who will be kings and priests with Christ and who will rule during that thousand years to bring blessings to mankind. This kingly governing body will be a heavenly group and is restricted in number to 144,000 persons.*[23]

THEOCRATIC DIRECTION TODAY

13 God's visible organization today also receives theocratic guidance and direction.

At the headquarters of Jehovah's Witnesses in Brooklyn, New York, there is a governing body of older Christian men from various parts of the earth who give the needed oversight to the worldwide activities of God's people. This governing body is made up of members of "the faithful and discreet slave." It serves as a spokesman for that faithful "slave."

14 The men of that governing body, like the apostles and older men in Jerusalem, have many years of experience in God's service. But they do not rely on human wisdom in making decisions. No, being governed theocratically, they follow the example of the early governing body in Jerusalem, whose decisions were based on God's Word and were made under the direction of holy spirit.—Acts 15:13-17, 28, 29.[24]

Knowing the three divisions in the book of Revelation is the key to forming this checkmate. Two verses, taken together, make it absolutely clear that the 144,000 falls into the future: Revelation 1:19 and Revelation 4:1.

Revelation 1:19 –
Write the things which thou hast seen [past tense], *and the things which are* [present tense], *and the things which shall be here-*

after [future tense]....

A three-fold division of time is presented in Revelation 1:19, as a three-fold division of the events of the Revelation itself.

- In Chapter 1 – John saw Christ unveiled in His ascended glory. This marks the first division, which is past.
- In Chapters 2 and 3 – John saw the seven churches. This marks the second division, which is in John's present time.
- In Chapter 4 – John is told to write those things which shall be hereafter. That marks the third division, which would be future.

Revelation 4:1 –
After this I looked, and, behold, a door was opened in heaven: and the first voice which I heard was as it were of a trumpet talking with me; which said, Come up hither, and I will shew thee things which must be hereafter [future].

Once you have asked the JW to read these key verses and have had him identify the three divisions, the following two questions will create the checkmate:

1. "Since the book of Revelation was written

about 90 A.D. and all of the events after Chapter 4 are future (the 144,000 are mentioned in chapters 7 and 14 of the Revelation), how could the disciples and the thousands of people saved at Pentecost and in the first century be numbered with the 144,000 anointed Christians when it was and still is, today, a future event?"

2. "Since the events described in Chapters 6-18 (please be aware that Armageddon takes place in Chapter 19, when Christ returns and begins His 1000-year reign) occur during the great tribulation period, which is yet future, how could anyone today claim to be one of the 144,000?"

The Watchtower also links the members of its governing body (8 to 12 leaders in Brooklyn) to the "Faithful and Discrete Slave" of Matthew 24:44-51, "whom Jesus appointed in 1919." Yet, in the same chapter, those chosen as faithful servants are rewarded at His coming after the seven-year great tribulation period described in Revelation chapters 6-18.

18 Yes, when the Master arrived, he found his faithful slave conscientiously feeding the domestics as well as preaching the good news. Greater responsibilities now awaited that slave. Jesus said: "Truly I say to you, He will appoint him over all his belongings." (Matthew 24:47) **Jesus did this in 1919,** *after the slave had passed through a period of testing. Why, though, did "the faithful and discreet slave" receive greater responsibilities? Because the Master had received an increase in his belongings. Jesus was given the kingship in 1914.*[25]

That those faithful servants are rewarded *after* rather than *during* the seven-years of tribulation is important. The Watchtower has them rewarded *during* (as quoted in the Watchtower's October 6, 2012 Annual Meeting Report).

Jesus' appointment of the "slave" over his "belongings," then, must also be a future event. He will make that appointment during the great tribulation.[26]

Matthew 24:1 –
For then shall be great tribulation, such as was not since the beginning of the world to this time, no, nor ever shall be.

Matthew 24:29 –
Immediately after the tribulation of those days shall the sun be darkened, and the moon shall not give her light, and the stars

> *shall fall from heaven, and the powers of the heavens shall be shaken:*
>
> Matthew 24:44 –
> *Therefore be ye also ready: for in such an hour as ye think not the Son of man **cometh**.*

The Son of man will come (*cometh*) after the great tribulation that ends in Revelation 19, at Armageddon. The 144,000 are identified in the events that will take place during the great tribulation period. The great tribulation begins with the future events described in 1 Thessalonians 4:13-18. Since these two things are so, it is not possible for anyone to claim to be a part of this group now. This means that neither the Watchtower leaders of the past, nor the Watchtower leaders of today can be members of the 144,000 mentioned in Revelation 7 and 14.

If you can make this truth clear to a JW, he will begin his journey away from the Watchtower organization. You have the ability to use this truth to lead JWs to the Christ, and you will be greatly blessed for so doing. The truth will set them free!

Remember, the goal is to end your conversation with the JW with his knowing that he is lost without any hope. Every encounter with a JW requires the Holy Spirit's leadership in both you and the JW. It is not possible to do this on your own. You must remain calm and un-intimidated, no matter where the dialogue leads. Preparation, prayer, and the power of the Holy Spirit is the combination that will result in a fruitful presentation of the gospel.

An attitude of prayer is the hidden strength that places the servant of the Lord in a position of absolute confidence. Think of the promise of Proverbs 3:6, "In all thy ways acknowledge him, and he shall direct thy paths." You must take this promise with you into every individual encounter of witnessing. Confidence will come from acting with faith upon the Lord's instructions. Mormons and JWs, though often perceived in the wrong way, can be engaged in meaningful dialogue through the power of the Spirit of God.

In every religious cult there are two groups: villains and victims. The cult leaders are the villains; the people they deceive are the victims. One would have great compassion for victims in a burning building and, in many instances, might risk his own life to save them. On the other hand, that same individual would have a feeling of rage for the villain who set the building on fire. This same contrast is what we must feel for a JW or a Mormon trapped in the burning building of deceit.

The Lord gave us these verses to remind His servants how to behave themselves when witnessing to the cults:

> 2 Timothy 2:24-26 –
> *24 And the servant of the Lord must not strive; but be gentle unto all men, apt to teach, patient,*
> *25 In meekness instructing those that oppose themselves; if God per-adventure will give them repentance to the acknowledging of the truth;*
> *26 And that they may recover themselves out of the snare of the devil, who are taken captive by him at his will.*

Do not be afraid of learning from your failures. Each encounter will make future witnessing to JWs more fruitful if you will learn from your failures. Over the twenty-plus years that I have been witnessing to JWs, I have failed many times. However, my burden to help a lost and dying soul has kept me from giving up.

Once the Lord gives you the joy of leading a JW to salvation, that JW will become one of your greatest resources in learning how to reach others. The Michael dialog, as simple as it is, is powerful. May the sweet Lord Jesus help you to use it effectively!

The JW's Last Stand Checkmate

After witnessing to JWs for many years, I have learned to expect the unexpected. Sometimes a JW is trying to eliminate all his lingering doubts about the One God who is Triune. If he is still using Watchtower literature as a source to find arguments that will contradict the Trinity, he will most certainly use the Watchtower's ultimate weapon by asking you this question: "How could the Trinity be true if John 17:3 is true?"

> John 17:3 –
> *And this is life eternal, that they might know thee the only true God, and Jesus Christ, whom thou hast sent.*

Notice how the verse is worded: "...the only true God, and Jesus Christ...." It appears to separate Jesus Christ from "the only true God." This is the ultimate weapon in the JWs attempt to deny the Trinity.

The Watchtower tries to use this verse in the same way that Mormons use their testimony, the "burning of the bosom." The wording in John 17:3 leaves a JW with the feeling of ultimate victory over anyone who believes that Jesus is God. JWs are told by Watchtower leaders that, in using this verse, they will checkmate any Christian who believes in the Trinity. The key to understanding what this verse is saying and what this verse is not saying is found in the word "true."

Consider what John 17:3 is not saying.

1. That the Father is the only God
2. That God the Son and God the Holy Spirit are not part of what God is
3. That Jesus is not God the Son

First, it is not saying that the Father is the only God. The Father sent the Son to be the Saviour of the world. As the Saviour, Jesus Christ is described as "the only wise God." This does not mean that the Father is not also God.

> 1 John 4:14 –
> *And we have seen and do testify that the Father sent the Son to be the Saviour of the world.*

> Jude 1:25 –
> *To the only wise God our Saviour, be glory and majesty, dominion and power, both now and ever. Amen.*

Second, John 17:3 is not saying that God the Son and God the Holy Spirit are not part of what God is. Jesus Himself gave a clear statement of the unity of the Godhead when He commanded believers to be baptized in the name (not *names*) of the Father, the Son and the Holy Spirit.

> Matthew 28:19 –
> *Go ye therefore, and teach all nations, baptizing them in the name of the Father, and of the Son, and of the Holy Ghost.*

Third, John 17:3 is not saying that Jesus is not God the Son. Jesus is saying that the Father, in comparison to all the false gods of the world, is the only true God. It is as simple as that!

Jesus is not comparing Himself to the Father in this verse. The main thought of John 17:3 has to do with what life eternal is. Jesus merely said that life eternal is this: knowing both the Father and the Son.

When Jesus speaks of knowing the Father and His Eternal Son, the Lord speaks of a personal, intimate relationship through the indwelling presence of God's Spirit. One could take in knowledge about God all his life and never know Him personally. However, knowing Him through salvation is life eternal.

> 1 John 5:20 –
> *And we know that the Son of God is come,*

> *and hath given us an understanding, that we may know him that is true, and we are in him that is true, even in his Son Jesus Christ. This is the true God, and eternal life.*

Every truly born-again child of God can testify to this reality.

Understanding what John 17:3 is and is not saying will keep the truths in John 1:1-3 from being disavowed. Any JW who is truly looking for the truth about the one God, who is Triune, will benefit greatly by a sound, contextual exposition of this verse.

Jehovah is *Jesus*

At some point, a Jehovah's Witness must be willing to except the Scriptural truth about the divinity of Jesus Christ. Many verses identify Jehovah as Jesus. One example of this truth has already been dealt with extensively, John 1:1. Consider examples from the book of Zechariah and the book of Psalms. From these examples, you will note the following:

1. John 1:1a – that Jesus is divine and, therefore, eternal.

2. Zechariah 12:10 and 14:3-4 – that Jehovah

is identified as Jesus and that Jehovah is eternal and divine.

3. Psalm 110:1 (and Matthew 22:45) – that Jehovah is both LORD and Lord: He is both divine and human.

Regarding John

John 1:1 –
In the beginning was the Word, and the Word was with God, and the Word was God.

An exposition of John 1:1 was made earlier in the book (beginning on page 30). The divinity of Christ is clearly shown in the sentence structure of the verse, as well as divinely revealed by these inspired words: "*and the Word was with God, and the Word was God.*" When a JW is willing to accept the authority of Scripture and to take God at His Word, the divinity of Christ will become a reality to him.

Regarding Zechariah

Zechariah 12:10 –
And I [Jehovah is speaking] *will pour upon the house of David, and upon the inhabitants of Jerusalem, the spirit of grace and of*

> *supplications: and they shall look upon me* [Jehovah] *whom they have pierced....*

When was Jehovah "pierced"? He was pierced when he hung on the cross of Calvary (John 19:34).

> Zechariah 14:3-4 –
> *Then shall the Lord* [Jehovah] *go forth, and fight against those nations* [this is Armageddon], *as when he fought in the day of battle. 4 And his feet* [Who's feet? Jehovah's/Jesus'] *shall stand in that day upon the mount of Olives, which is before Jerusalem on the east, and the mount of Olives shall cleave in the midst thereof toward the east and toward the west....*

Whose feet shall stand on the Mount of Olives? It will be Jesus, who is Jehovah. He will return to this earth to reign forever (Rev. 19:11-17)!

When a JW sees and understands from Scripture that Jehovah is Jesus, he will see Christ's divinity. He will no longer accept the Watchtower's false teaching that the Father is Jehovah and Jesus is Michael the archangel, Jehovah's first created being.

Regarding Psalms

Psalm 110:1 –
The Lord said unto my Lord, Sit thou at my right hand, until I make thine enemies thy footstool.

The Lord used Psalm 110:1 to baffle the Pharisees by posing a question that exhibited the Messiah's divinity. When a JW is asked this same question, he is compelled to answer it by believing in the divinity of Christ. Matthew records the scene (Matthew 22:42-45).

After answering several questions designed to entangle Him in His talk, the Lord asks the Pharisees a question of His own: "What think ye of Christ? Whose son is he?"

Their reply (that Christ is "the Son of David") leads the Lord to ask, "How then doth David in spirit call him Lord, saying, The LORD said unto my Lord, Sit thou on my right hand, till I make thine enemies thy footstool? If David then call him Lord, how is he his son?"

What is the answer to the Lord's question, "If David then call him Lord, how is he his son"? How does Psalm 110:1 prophesy of Christ?

The answer is found in the uniqueness of Jesus Christ. Psalm 110:1 is a prophecy. It is a prophecy of both Christ's divinity and His humanity:

1. Christ's divinity: Christ, as God, was David's LORD.

2. Christ's humanity: Christ, as Man, was David's Son.

CHAPTER 5: The God Question

The term Godhead, more commonly referred to as the Trinity, represents one eternal God. He is Triune and exists in three eternal persons: God the Father, God the Son, and God the Holy Spirit. They are perfect in unity, equal in nature, distinct in person, and subordinate in duties. This means that God has three parts: each part is fully God, and there is only one God.

Jesus, as the eternal Son of God, is eternally begotten by the Father and is submissive to do His work; yet, He is equal in essence and nature to God the Father. The Apostle Paul writes the church at Corinth concerning this headship.

> 1 Corinthians 11:3 –
> *But I would have you know, that the head of every man is Christ; and the head of the woman is the man; and the head of Christ is God.*

Consider this question: "Because the man was over the woman, did this make the woman inferior to the man?" The answer is, "No." The woman is not inferior to the man. Neither would the Headship of the Father make the Son or the Holy Spirit inferior to the Father. The role of subjection creates unity and harmony within the Godhead, as well as in the order of all God's creation.

God the Father is the voice of authority; God the Son is the channel of authority; God the Holy Spirit is the agent of authority. This relationship (voice, channel and agent) is the reason why the Bible can say that God created all things, Jesus created all things and the Holy Spirit quickens (gives life to) all things without the Bible contradicting itself. The will of God remains in perfect unity and harmony with each member of the Godhead at all times.

>Genesis 1:1 –
>*In the beginning God* [God the Father, God the Son, and God the Holy Spirit] *created the heaven and the earth.*
>
>Genesis 1:2 –
>*And the earth was without form, and void; and darkness was upon the face of the deep. And the Spirit of God moved upon the face of the waters.*
>
>John 1:3 –
>*All things were made by him* [Jesus Christ]*; and without him was not anything made that was made.*
>
>Colossians 1:16 –

For by him [Jesus Christ] *were all things created, that are in heaven, and that are in earth, visible and invisible, whether they be thrones, or dominions, or principalities, or powers: all things were created by him, and for him:*

The Bible declares that God created all things, that Jesus created all things, and that the Holy Spirit quickens all things. It does so without contradiction, by the relationship of the three persons of the Trinity.

Since Jesus is God, with God (John 1:1-3), having no beginning nor ending, Jesus was never created. With this in mind, consider the following statement: the first created was never the firstborn. Adam and Eve were the first created.

Regarding Firstborn & First Created

First, we must understand the difference between the term "first created" and the term "firstborn." Second, we must make a distinction between the two applications of the term "firstborn": in one sense it is to be taken literally; in another sense it is used figuratively. The Bible clearly states that the first created humans were Adam and Eve.

Genesis 1:27 –

So God created man in his own image, in the image of God created he him; male and female created he them.

JWs try to use the term *firstborn* to prove that Jesus is a created being. Their error is in using the word literally in Colossians 1:15-18, when the word *firstborn* is used figuratively in this passage. Used literally, *firstborn* means "the one who is born (from within its mother) first." Used figuratively, it means "the one who has the preeminence over all others."

To understand Colossians 1:15-18, one must know the difference between these two terms: "first created" and "firstborn," as well as the distinction made between the literal sense and the figurative sense of "firstborn."

Colossians 1:15-18 –
Who is the image of the invisible God, the firstborn of every creature:
16 For by him were all things created, that are in heaven, and that are in earth, visible and invisible, whether they be thrones, or dominions, or principalities, or powers: all things were created by him, and for him:
17 And he [Jesus Christ] *is before all things, and by him all things consist.*
18 And he is the head of the body, the

church: who is the beginning, the firstborn from the dead; that in all things he [Jesus Christ] *might have the preeminence.*

Consider the following "firstborn" sons:

1. Cain, the firstborn (the literal use of the term)
2. Ephraim, my firstborn (the figurative use of the term)

When the word *firstborn* is used literally in the Bible, it always means that someone or something is being born by virtue of a physical birth. Cain was the firstborn son of Adam and Eve. Therefore, Cain is called the firstborn.

Genesis 4:1 –
And Adam knew Eve his wife; and she conceived, and bare Cain, and said, I have gotten a man from the LORD.

When the word *firstborn* is used figuratively in the Bible, it always means that someone has been raised to a position of honor. There are numerous examples of God elevating a person to the position of preeminence, calling him the *firstborn* because of that position. The following two examples illustrate this figurative use of the term *firstborn*:

1. Joseph's two sons, Manasseh and Ephraim
2. Jesse's youngest son, David

Joseph – sold by his brethren, but sustained by the Lord – is given Asenath, the daughter of Potipherah, priest of On, in Egypt, to wed. She bears two sons of Joseph: Manasseh and Ephraim.

> Genesis 41:50-52 –
> *And unto Joseph were born two sons before the years of famine came, which Asenath the daughter of Potipherah priest of On bare unto him.*
> *51 And Joseph called the name of the firstborn Manasseh: For God, said he, hath made me forget all my toil, and all my father's house.*
> *52 And the name of the second called he Ephraim: For God hath caused me to be fruitful in the land of my affliction.*

Ephraim, who is clearly the second born, is later said to be the firstborn. This is positional, and the term *firstborn* is used figuratively of Ephraim.

> Jeremiah 31:9 –
> *They shall come with weeping, and with supplications will I lead them: I will cause them to walk by the rivers of waters in a straight way, wherein they shall not*

> *stumble: for I am a father to Israel, and Ephraim is my firstborn.*

Jesse has eight sons. When Samuel is sent to the house of Jesse to anoint the next king of Israel, Jesse brings his firstborn son, Eliab, before the prophet. Samuel looks at him and thinks, "Surely the Lord's anointed is before him" (1 Samuel 16:6). But the Lord had refused Eliab because God looks on the heart. Samuel has to go through the first seven sons of Jesse before the prophet is told that there is one who is the youngest and he is out keeping the sheep (2 Samuel 16:11).

David was the last of eight sons, but the LORD ranks him figuratively as the firstborn!

> Psalm 89:27 –
> *Also I will make him* [David] *my firstborn, higher than the kings of the earth.*

Any honest student of the Bible must ask himself whether the term *firstborn* in Colossians 1:15-18 is used literally or figuratively. If it is used literally, then in the pre-existence Jesus must have had a mom and a dad when he was born from the womb. Is this what verse 15 is saying?

> Colossians 1:15 –
> *Who is the image of the invisible God, the*

firstborn of every creature:

No, that would be absurd! Also, one cannot be literally born from the dead, for a literal birth only takes place when one is born from the womb. When the term *firstborn* is used figuratively, it denotes "first in rank or preeminence," which is precisely what the Scripture is saying in Colossians 1:15-18.

The term *firstborn,* used in verse 15, signifies one's position. In the same way the firstborn child in a family is born before his siblings, likewise Christ existed before creation. The firstborn of any family was customarily given more honors, greater authority, and a larger share of the inheritance than the other children in that family.

Christ, as the firstborn of every creature – it is clear that the figurative sense of the term is used here – is before, as well as pre-eminent in all creation. The reason for His pre-eminence is clearly explained in the passage itself. Look again at Colossians 1:16 –

> *For by him* [Jesus Christ] *were all things created....*

Continuing in that passage, note the following:

> Verse 17 –
> *And he is before all things*
>
> Verse 18 –
> *...who is the beginning...*

Jesus Christ is the beginning in the sense that He is the source and origin of all things. This is the precise meaning of the word *beginning* as used in the Revelation.

> Revelation 3:14 –
> *These things saith the Amen* [Jesus Christ], *the faithful and true witness, the beginning* [the source or origin] *of the creation of God.*

The positional pre-eminence of Christ in the resurrection is amplified in Colossians 1:18 by the figurative use of the term *firstborn from the dead*. Christ has the pre-eminence in the resurrection because He is the firstfruits of the resurrection.

> 1 Corinthians 15:20 –
> *But now is Christ risen from the dead, and become the firstfruits of them that slept.*

What about Proverbs 8:22? Is it saying that Jesus was created?

> Proverbs 8:22 –

> *The LORD possessed me* [wisdom] *in the beginning of his way, before his works of old.*

If you believe that the context of a passage of Scripture determines the meaning of what is being said, the answer is, "Absolutely not!" Proverbs 8:22 does not say that Jesus was created! Jesus has always been!

Proverbs 8 is comparing the wicked woman of chapter seven to the spiritual woman of chapter eight. *Wisdom* is personified in chapter eight as a woman prophetess. Look at the feminine pronouns in the beginning of the chapter: *her voice...she standeth...she crieth....*

> Proverbs 8:1-3 —
> *Doth not wisdom cry? and understanding put forth her voice?*
> *2 She standeth in the top of high places, by the way in the places of the paths.*
> *3 She crieth at the gates, at the entry of the city, at the coming in at the doors.*

When we come to verse 22 of the chapter, we find that God is simply emphasizing His use of wisdom as His basic principle in creating the universe.

CHAPTER 6: The *Heaven* Question

The heaven question falls into the category of Bible doctrine called *eschatology*, which is better known as "the study of the last things or last days." It is a vital part of leaving a Mormon or JW with the understanding from Scripture that they are lost and without any hope. It is vital to leading them to hope in Christ.

To many people, the word "heaven" is used as a term that represents the positive side of life after death, without reference to any particular place, condition, or duration of time. To Mormons and JWs, the word "heaven" still represents the positive side of life. But they each have an unscriptural view about heaven, and they each have a view that is very different doctrinally from the other.

What both have in common is this: that neither Mormons nor JWs have a view of the Eternal Kingdom of God. This is the Kingdom of Righteousness, which begins in Revelation 21. This is the Kingdom view that agrees with Scripture and follows the rules of context and harmony.

Remember, without the referees of context and harmony, anything goes. However, with these two rules applied to Scripture, there is no wiggle-room for the cults (or anyone else) to deny or distort Scripture. Knowing what Mormons and JWs believe about heaven and knowing what the Scripture teaches about heaven, you will be able to create a checkmate in their minds as you witness for Christ.

What Do Mormons Teach About Heaven?

Mormons believe in three levels of heaven. The more holy one's life is on earth, the higher the level of heaven one can enjoy. A holier life here means enjoying better conditions there.

Before getting into the specifics about what Mormons teach regarding heaven, consider some Bible terms that are used when speaking about the afterlife (life after death): *heaven, the eternal state, the kingdom of righteousness, the eternal kingdom, hell,* and *the lake of fire.* These terms take on a meaning different from the Bible when used by cultists, as you will see in the quotes from Mormon prophets.

Ed Decker is an ex-Mormon, who served as a temple Mormon, an elder in the Melchizedek priesthood (the highest priesthood) and a teacher. He held positions of authority for 20 years in the Mormon Church. Decker gives a brief overview;

then, he quotes from *Doctrine and Covenants* (one of the four books the Mormons view as scripture). This is what Decker has to say about the Mormon heavens:

The LDS Position

The highest kingdom of degree of glory for the resurrected person is the celestial glory or celestial kingdom. The celestial kingdom is reserved for those Mormons who have lived lives of purity and obedience to all the laws and ordinances of the LDS "gospel" throughout his or her lifetime. There are three levels of glory within the celestial kingdom. There are some general theories as to how they are divided and peopled, but the official doctrine is this:

1 In the celestial glory there are three heavens or degrees; 2 And in order to obtain the highest, a man must enter into this order of the priesthood (LSD note—not the author's); [meaning the new and everlasting covenant of marriage]; 3 And if he does not, he cannot obtain it. 4 He may enter into the other, but that is the end of his kingdom; he cannot have an increase.[27]

To a Mormon, heaven (that is, the celestial heaven)

is equal to "full salvation" and is synonymous with exaltation (when a man is promoted to a god and can produce spirit children who later will be born as physical children). The following are two quotes from the Mormon book, *Gospel Principles*.

Quote #1:

> *Blessings of Exaltation*
>
> *Our Heavenly Father is perfect. However, he is not jealous of his wisdom and perfection. He glories in the fact that it is possible for his children to become like him. He has said, "This is my work and my glory—to bring to pass the immortality and eternal life of man" (Moses 1:39).*
>
> *Those who receive exaltation in the celestial kingdom through faith in Jesus Christ will receive special blessings. The Lord has promised, "All things are theirs" (D&C 76:59). These are some of the blessings given to exalted people:*
>
> *1. They will live eternally in the presence of Heavenly Father and Jesus Christ (see D&C 76).*
> *2. They will become gods.*

3. They will have their righteous family members with them and will be able to have spirit children also. These spirit children will have the same relationship to them as we do to our Heavenly Father. They will be an eternal family.
4. They will receive a fullness of joy.
5. They will have everything that our Heavenly Father and Jesus Christ have—all power, glory, dominion, and knowledge.

President Joseph Fielding Smith wrote: "The Father has promised through the Son that all that he has shall be given to those who are obedient to his commandments."[28]

Quote #2:

This is the way our Heavenly Father became God. Joseph Smith taught: "It is the first principle of the Gospel to know for a certainty the character of God. . . . He was once a man like us; ... God himself, the Father of us all, dwelt on an earth, the same as Jesus Christ himself did."[29]

Notice these two statements from the second quote:

1. "This is the way our Heavenly Father

became God."
2. "He was once a man like us."

The Mormon is told that the Heavenly Father became God and that he (God) was once a man. This is what the Mormon believes. How, then, could a Mormon ever come to the conclusion that what he has been told about the afterlife is not true? The answer to this question is in this Scripture:

> Romans 10:17 –
> *So then faith* [true faith] *cometh by hearing, and hearing by the word of God.*

Have you ever spoken with an ex-Mormon or ex-JW, one who has been truly saved? If you get that opportunity, he will say that it was the Bible that led him to freedom in Christ. One must believe that the truth of God's Word, as given in the Bible, is the power of God unto salvation.

Our task is to show Mormons and JWs the conflicts between the false revelations and "new light" of their leaders and the truth of God's Word. Once we do that, the Lord will do the rest through His Spirit and His Word.

People who really want to know the truth will be

willing to take God at His Word. Those who reject His Word will be eternally lost. The checkmate is like sowing the good seed: all it needs is the right soil.

> Luke 8:15 –
> *But that on the good ground are they, which in an honest and good heart, having heard the word, keep it, and bring forth fruit with patience.*

When talking with a Mormon, remember to ask him if he believes that the King James Bible is God's Word. He most likely has a copy on him, in his briefcase or back-pack, or near him in his home. He will probably say, "Yes, that which is translated correctly."

What does he mean when he says, "If it is translated correctly"? Here is your answer. He will say the following:

> *We believe the Bible to be the word of God as far as it is translated correctly; we also believe the Book of Mormon to be the word of God.*[30]

John 1:3 is the checkmate verse. It is the checkmate because the Mormon's false-Jesus comes into existence after creation of the universe.

To my knowledge, no Mormon rewriting of the Scripture has changed that verse.

> *All things were made by him; and without him was not anything made which was made (John 1:3 JST).*

Any attempt that a Mormon may make to avoid or to refute the truth that the Mormon Jesus is a false Jesus is refuted by this verse. Jesus could not have come into existence as a spirit-son of the Mormon Heavenly Father and be the Creator of everything that exists. The Bible says that He is the Creator of everything that exists.

The Mormon must be shown that it is not possible for him to go to heaven by his good works or his desire. Desire and good works do not open heaven unto us; faith in Jesus Christ opens heaven to us. One cannot believe in a false Jesus and a false god and have true salvation.

The claim by cultists that the Bible has been corrupted is an attempt to undermine its authority. The Devil did the same thing in the garden with Eve. He declared, *"Yea, hath God said"* and *"Ye shall not surely die" (Genesis 3:1c; 4b).*

The Mormon statement – *as far as it is translated correctly* – generates doubt in God's Word. The

Mormon writings, claiming to be inspired, only serve to contradict what God has truly said. What has God truly said? *Ye shall surely die.*

This has been the battle throughout the ages. Many have fallen victim to the Devils' lie; however, many Mormons and JWs have been delivered. Do not give up! Get ready for the conflict, knowing that all who are willing to take God at His Word will be saved.

What Do JWs Teach About Heaven?

Watchtower followers are taught that only a small number of people are chosen for heaven. All the rest are told that, if they endure until the end and stay loyal to Jehovah's organization, they will be resurrected at Armageddon. Then, they will be on probation during the millennial kingdom. All those who remain faithful until the end will receive everlasting life and remain on earth.

This is not all that the Watchtower (WT) teaches about the afterlife. There are numerous other flaws in the way they spiritualize Scripture and make applications that do not come from its context. But this is the heart of their teaching.

> *2 The wrathful nations, though resorting to totalitarian methods, are unable to drown*

out Jehovah's praise. In fulfillment of Revelation 19:6 our ears can hear what is as the "voice of a great crowd and as a sound of many waters and as a sound of heavy thunders". Yes, we can hear them saying: "Praise Jah, you people, because Jehovah our God, the Almighty, has begun to rule as king." (NW) Since the sound of their voices is so mighty that it is likened to the sound of many waters and to thunder peals, terrestrial and celestial sounds, it suggests that an earthly class and a heavenly class are producing the mighty proclamation. The facts agree with this. The remnant of spiritual Israelites who are in line for the heavenly kingdom have been openly praising Jah or Jehovah since A.D. 1919, when they were released from Babylon's power. They have since been joined by hundreds of thousands of believers whose hope is for an earthly destiny in the new world.[31]

32 This does not conflict with the heavenly hope that God puts in the hearts of the followers of Jesus Christ. These God makes his spiritual children by the use of his holy spirit or active force, to start them in a new way of life, a heavenly life. These comparatively few Christians, pictured by the twenty-four "elders" in the vision to John, are said to be begotten or engendered by God through the means of his life-giving spirit. So they set their affections and keep their minds fixed on the things above. In the resurrection from the dead they expect to be born like Jesus Christ into the fullness of spirit life in heaven, changed, transformed indeed.—1 Cor. 15:42-54.

33 The heavenly hope of these 144,000 faithful ones of the true Christian congregation does not leave the rest of mankind with nothing to hope for. That gleaming hope of an earthly Paradise, where God's will is to be done on earth as well as in heaven, is the blessed hope reserved for them according to God's unchanged loving purpose. The realizing of the heavenly hope by the faithful, world-conquering congregation of Christ takes place before the realizing of the earthly hope by faithful men of pre-Christian times and by faithful men of good will toward Jehovah God today. The realizing of the heavenly hope by the Christian congregation also works for the realizing of the earthly hope by believers of mankind.[32]

Followers of the Watchtower publications are also

taught that people who are lost will have a second chance to be saved after the Great White Throne judgment. These are those individuals who never accepted the Watchtower's message. If that were true, why would someone ever become a JW in the first place?

> *According to the apostle John's vision, "scrolls were opened," and "the dead were judged out of those things written in the scrolls according to their deeds." Are these scrolls the record of people's past deeds? No, the judgment will not focus on what people did before they died. How do we know that? The Bible says: "He who has died has been acquitted from his sin." (Romans 6:7) Those resurrected thus come to life with a clean slate, so to speak. The scrolls must therefore represent God's further requirements. To live forever, both Armageddon survivors and resurrected ones will have to obey God's commandments, including whatever new requirements Jehovah might reveal during the thousand years. Thus, individuals will be judged on the basis of what they do during Judgment Day.*
>
> *By the end of Judgment Day, surviving humans will have "come to life" fully as*

perfect humans. (Revelation 20:5) Judgment Day will thus see the restoration of mankind to its original perfect state. (1 Corinthians 15:24-28) Then a final test will take place. Satan will be released from his imprisonment and allowed to try to mislead mankind one last time. (Revelation 20:3, 7-10) Those who resist him will enjoy the complete fulfillment of the Bible's promise: "The righteous themselves will possess the earth, and they will reside forever upon it." (Psalm 37:29) Yes, Judgment Day will be a blessing to all faithful mankind.[33]

What Does the Bible Teach?

1. God's Heaven (the third heaven) was created for His dwelling place.
2. God's Heaven is the current home of all the redeemed.
3. God's Heavenly City, the New Jerusalem (where He will dwell forever) comes down to a newly created earth, where all whose names are written in the Lamb's book of life will dwell with Him eternally.

The cults have a view of heaven that has been twisted and obscured by the vain imaginations of their false prophets and false teachers, their so-called "anointed-ones." The authority of Scripture comes from its context. Once a truth is stated, it will not contradict itself. With that in mind, look at God's eternal abiding place and see what He has said.

Heaven: God's Present Dwelling Place

> 1 Kings 8:30 –
> *And hearken thou to the supplication of thy servant, and of thy people Israel, when they shall pray toward this place: and hear thou in heaven thy dwelling place: and when thou hearest, forgive.*

> Psalm 11:4 –
> *The LORD is in his holy temple, the LORD'S throne is in heaven: his eyes behold, his eyelids try, the children of men.*

> Matthew 18:10 –
> *Take heed that ye despise not one of these little ones; for I say unto you, That in heaven their angels do always behold the face of my Father which is in heaven.*

God's "dwelling place" is in heaven. Notice, now, which heaven.

> 2 Corinthians 12:2-4 –
> *I knew a man in Christ above fourteen years*

ago, (whether in the body, I cannot tell; or whether out of the body, I cannot tell: God knoweth;) such an one caught up to the third heaven.
3 And I knew such a man, (whether in the body, or out of the body, I cannot tell: God knoweth;)
4 How that he was caught up into paradise, and heard unspeakable words, which it is not lawful for a man to utter.

The Apostle Paul was caught up to the "third heaven." To have a "third," we must have a first and second.

1. The First Heaven is "the open heaven," where the fowls fly (Genesis 1:20).
2. The Second Heaven is "space," where the lights divide the day from the night (Genesis 1:14).
3. The Third Heaven is where God dwells now (2 Corinthians 12:24).

Heaven: Present Home of the Redeemed

John 17:24 –
Father, I will that they also, whom thou hast given me, be with me where I am; that they may behold my glory, which thou hast given me: for thou lovedst me before the foun-

dation of the world.

2 Corinthians 5:8 –
We are confident, I say, and willing rather to be absent from the body, and to be present with the Lord.

Philippians 1:23 –
For I am in a strait betwixt two, having a desire to depart, and to be with Christ; which is far better.

The Redeemed who have left this life in death are with the Lord.

1 Thessalonians 3:13 –
To the end he may stablish your hearts unblameable in holiness before God, even our Father, at the coming of our Lord Jesus Christ with all his saints.

1 Thessalonians 4:16-17 –
*For the Lord himself shall descend from heaven with a shout, with the voice of the archangel, and with the trump of God: and the dead in Christ shall rise first:
17 Then we which are alive and remain shall be caught up together with them in the clouds, to meet the Lord in the air: and so shall we ever be with the Lord.*

When the Lord Jesus Christ returns to this earth, the Redeemed who are with Him in heaven will return with Him to earth.

> Revelation 5:3 –
> *And no man in heaven, nor in earth, neither under the earth* [in hell], *was able to open the book, neither to look thereon.*
>
> Revelation 7:13-15 –
> *And one of the elders answered, saying unto me, What are these which are arrayed in white robes? and whence came they?*
> *14 And I said unto him, Sir, thou knowest. And he said to me, These are they which came out of great tribulation, and have washed their robes, and made them white in the blood of the Lamb.*
> *15 Therefore are they before the throne of God, and serve him day and night in his temple: and he that sitteth on the throne shall dwell among them.*

The group returning with the Lord includes those "which came out of great tribulation," the "little season" (Rev. 6:11). Together with the brethren of the tribulation's first period, these are slain for the word of God (Rev. 6:9-11). They are redeemed as all are redeemed: "Made white in the blood of the Lamb." Thank the Lord for Calvary!

Heaven: The New Jerusalem, the New Earth

The New Jerusalem will be God's eternal dwelling place. The New Earth will be man's eternal dwelling place. The new creation will be heaven on earth.

> *Christ said, "In my Father's house are many mansions" (John 14:2). The "Father's house" is no less than the universe in which there are many abodes.*[34]

> *Considering the fact that the new heavens and the new earth will be the eternal abode of the saints, it is remarkable that there is comparatively little description of it in the entire Scripture.*[35]

> *The New Earth is the ultimate Promised Land, the eternal Holy Land in which all God's people will dwell.*[36]

In my Father's house is a reference to God's dwelling place. When Christ spoke of His Father's house in John 14:2, the book of Revelation had not been written. The only other mention of *my Father's house* by the Saviour is recorded in John 2:16. It was a reference to the temple in Jerusalem. God said that His eternal dwelling place would be in Zion, which is Jerusalem. Jesus also said that His kingdom (the eternal kingdom of righteousness) was not of this world. It was not of this world because it was a reference to the new heaven and new earth that He would create after this present heaven and earth would be destroyed by fire.

The new earth and new heaven is the *place* Jesus promised to prepare for His sheep, the sheep whose names are written in the Lamb's book of life. The splendor of this new earth will be Christ Himself. He will descend from heaven, robed in the beauty of the Heavenly Jerusalem as it comes down to earth. He will show each of His own their new home and all the glories of His kingdom of righteousness.

Jesus referred to the Temple in Jerusalem as "my Father's house."

> John 2:16 –
> *And said unto them that sold doves, Take these things hence; make not my Father's house an house of merchandise.*

As the Father's "house" (verse 16), the Temple is described as God's dwelling place.

> John 14:2 –
> *In my Father's house are many mansions: if*

it were not so, I would have told you. I go to prepare a place for you.

Can you imagine all the redeemed standing on the newly created earth (God's dwelling place or the Father's house) and viewing the New Jerusalem coming down from the sky? Can you imagine seeing Jesus Christ with a radiance so bright that it illuminates the entire city?

Though God will destroy the earth and its works by fire, we look for a new earth.

2 Peter 3:10 –
But the day of the Lord will come as a thief in the night; in the which the heavens shall pass away with a great noise, and the elements shall melt with fervent heat, the earth also and the works that are therein shall be burned up.

2 Peter 3:13 –
Nevertheless we, according to his promise, look for new heavens and a new earth, wherein dwelleth righteousness.

Isaiah 65:17 –
For, behold, I create new heavens and a new earth: and the former shall not be remembered, nor come into mind.

Those who will inhabit this new earth are described by the Lord with one term: *meek*.

> Psalm 37:11 –
> *But the meek shall inherit the earth; and shall delight themselves in the abundance of peace.*

The word *meek* stands for all those whose names are written in the Lamb's book of life.

> John 18:36 –
> *Jesus answered, My kingdom is not of this world: if my kingdom were of this world, then would my servants fight, that I should not be delivered to the Jews: but now is my kingdom not from hence.*

The promise of Christ's kingdom of righteousness that is not of this world has its fulfillment in Revelation 21, in the new earth and the New Jerusalem.

> Psalm 132:13-14 –
> *For the Lord hath chosen Zion; he hath desired it for his habitation.*
> *14 This is my rest for ever: here will I dwell; for I have desired it.*

This prophecy sets the stage for what will take

place in the New Jerusalem. *Zion* is a word used for Jerusalem in the Old Testament. There, God will rest forever.

Revelation 21:1-4 –
And I saw a new heaven and a new earth: for the first heaven and the first earth were passed away; and there was no more sea.
2 And I John saw the holy city, new Jerusalem, coming down from God out of heaven, prepared as a bride adorned for her husband.
3 And I heard a great voice out of heaven saying, Behold, the tabernacle of God is with men, and he will dwell with them, and they shall be his people, and God himself shall be with them, and be their God.
4 And God shall wipe away all tears from their eyes; and there shall be no more death, neither sorrow, nor crying, neither shall there be any more pain: for the former things are passed away.

Revelation 21:9-10 –
And there came unto me one of the seven angels which had the seven vials full of the seven last plagues, and talked with me, saying, Come hither, I will shew thee the bride, the Lamb's wife.
10 And he carried me away in the spirit to a

great and high mountain, and shewed me that great city, the holy Jerusalem, descending out of heaven from God.

Revelation 21 is the beginning of Christ's eternal kingdom of righteousness. One should seek it first above all things of this present world, for Jesus said that His kingdom was not of this world. It is the eternal home of the righteous, those who have been made clean by the blood of the Lamb.

If you have been born-again, I would like to invite you to visit my mansion that has been prepared just for me. Glory be to the Lamb, my Redeemer, who is worthy of power, riches, wisdom, strength, honor, glory and blessing. Amen!

Revelation 21:27 –
And there shall in no wise enter into it any thing that defileth, neither whatsoever worketh abomination, or maketh a lie: but they which are written in the Lamb's book of life.

Are you 100% sure that your name is written in the Lamb's book of life?

CHAPTER 7: The Hell Question

The hell question also falls into the category of Bible doctrine called *eschatology,* since the study of last things involves death, judgment, heaven (as reward) and hell (as punishment). There are many different ways to introduce the subject of *hell*; but, I can think of no better way than to say the following:

"Thank you, Lord Jesus, because I do not have to go there. Thank you for saving my wretched soul, for taking my place on that cursed tree and for birthing me into the family of God, just because I received you as my Saviour, God and King. I want to thank you that I will be like you, Jesus, someday and be with you forever to behold your glory!"

> John 17:24 –
> *Father, I will that they also, whom thou hast given me, be with me where I am; that they may behold my glory, which thou hast given me: for thou lovedst me before the foundation of the world.*

What Do Mormons Teach About Hell?

The Mormon book, *Gospel Principles*, has nothing listed for *hell* in its subject index. However, a short comment is made in the glossary. That comment is as follows:

> *The part of the spirit world where wicked spirits await the day of their resurrection; also the place where Satan and his followers dwell.*[37]

The Book of Mormon offers additional information in the form of one reference. That reference reads as follows:

> *Therefore if that man repenteth not, and remaineth and dieth an enemy to God, the demands of divine justice do awaken his immortal soul to a lively sense of his own guilt, which doth cause him to shrink from the presence of the Lord, and doth fill his breast with guilt, and pain, and anguish, which is like an unquenchable fire, whose flame ascendeth up forever and ever (Mosiah 2:38).*

A Google search yields more detailed explanations of the Mormon teachings on hell. The term is applied to stages, one of which is described as the "misery which may attend a person in mortality due to disobedience to divine law." This is another way of speaking of hell on earth. None of their stages portray what the Bible actually teaches. Note the following explanation:

What do Mormons believe about hell, and who is going there? Short answer: Mormons believe in hell, but our conception of hell is different than the one that generally springs to mind, and we use the word to mean different things in different contexts. For us, there are two "hells", really. One is a state of pain, guilt, and anguish where the spirits of the wicked will be after they die but before the final judgment (we often call this state spirit prison). The other is an everlasting state of hell reserved for a few truly wicked (we commonly refer to this one as outer darkness). Because the second state only applies to few, for the majority of people hell will not last forever: after the final judgment most people will receive some degree of glory.

Long answer: I wrote this post because I've found that people assume we believe in the traditional hellfire and damnation, and that causes a lot of misunderstanding. For instance, we claim to be the only religion with the "fullness of the gospel," and that you have to be baptized by someone authorized by God (only in the LDS church) in order to be saved. People hear that and assume that we therefore believe that everyone else is "going to hell" in the sense that most modern Christians would use the phrase. That isn't our belief, however.[38]

Their "spirit-prison" is a temporary state while they await resurrection. During this state, those who suffer there "are cleansed through suffering."[39] In reality, Hell neither cleanses nor purifies anyone.

When you see what the Bible teaches about Hell, you will have a clear understanding of how Mormons have changed Hell into a much more comfortable place. The JWs have done the same thing. Their teachings illustrate how Satan attempts to take the "sting" out of death by denying that death results in an everlasting torment that is both mental and physical.

What Do JWs Teach About Hell?

Jehovah's Witnesses, more specifically the Watchtower (WT) leaders, teach that *hell* is the common grave of mankind and that the soul and spirit are not immortal. Their teaching is called *conditionalism* or *annihilationism*. They hold to nonexistence (annihilation) after judgment and to soul-sleep between death and judgment.

The Watchtower's founder, Charles Taze Russell,

was greatly influenced by George Storrs. Storrs developed his ideas of the afterlife from reading a tract in 1837, written by "Deacon" Henry Grew, an English-born, ex-Baptist pastor from Philadelphia. Dr. M. James Penton, an ex-JW and Professor of History and Religious Studies at the University of Toronto, recorded this information in a book he wrote of the history on the WT movement entitled, *Apocalypse Delayed: The Story of Jehovah's Witnesses*.

Penton was a fourth generation JW. He was disfellowshipped in 1981. His book stands alone in its concise and factual history of the continuous changes that resulted from the men in the WT's leadership and how they developed a system of authority that enabled them to continuously say that the organization was being led by Jehovah, even when it is teaching error.

> *Of the two men who influenced Russell, George Storrs was by far the more important. Born in 1796 in Lebanon, New Hampshire, he, like Russell, was raised in a stern Calvinist environment. But at the age of twenty-nine, he became a convert to Methodism and later was ordained as a minister of the Methodist Episcopal Church....More important was the fact that in 1837 he read a tract by "Deacon" Henry*

> *Grew....From that tract Storrs came to believe in what is called "conditionalism," or "annihilationism."*[40]

Watchtower leaders have tried to support their "no hell doctrine" by taking issue with the translations that use the same English word for both *hell* and *grave*. This argument has much to do with the Hebrew and Greek words that mean "the place of departed spirits or souls of the dead." What they never mention is that the word for the burial place in the ground and the place of departed spirits are two different words in both Hebrew and Greek. Would it be possible that the reason this is not mentioned is that it would make their arguments void and null?

The following is an example of how the Watchtower treats the account of the rich man and Lazarus, taken from *You Can Live Forever in Paradise on Earth*.

THE RICH MAN AND LAZARUS

> *19 What, then, did Jesus mean when he said in one of his illustrations: "The beggar died, and was carried by the angels into Abraham's bosom: the rich man also died, and was buried; and in hell [Hades] he lift up his eyes, being in torments, and seeth*

Abraham afar off, and Lazarus in his bosom"? (Luke 16:19-31, King James Version) Since, as we have seen, Hades refers to mankind's grave, and not to a place of torment, it is plain that Jesus was here telling an illustration or a story. As further evidence that this is not a literal account but is an illustration, consider this: Is hell literally within speaking distance of heaven so that such a real conversation could be carried on? Moreover, if the rich man were in a literal burning lake, how could Abraham send Lazarus to cool his tongue with just a drop of water on the tip of his finger? What, then, was Jesus illustrating?

20 The rich man in the illustration stood for the self-important religious leaders who rejected Jesus and later killed him. Lazarus pictured the common people who accepted God's Son. The death of the rich man and of Lazarus represented a change in their condition. This change took place when Jesus fed the neglected Lazarus-like people spiritually, so that they thus came into the favor of the Greater Abraham, Jehovah God. At the same time, the false religious leaders "died" with respect to having God's favor. Being cast off, they suffered torments when Christ's followers exposed their evil

> works. *(Acts 7:51-57)* So this illustration does not teach that some dead persons are tormented in a literal fiery hell.[41]

What Does The Bible Teach About Hell?

The *Hell* question is answered clearly in the Sacred Text. Its doctrine centered around three main words and the teachings of Jesus Christ Himself. Those three words are the Hebrew word *sheol* and the Greek words *hades* and *gehenna*.

In the vernacular of our day, the word *hell* would often be used by common folks to mean any or all of these words. The Word of God, taken in its context, will prove that Hell is a place where there is a state of continuous existence and torment. The lake of fire is an expression that comes from the imagery of *gehenna* that pictures the final state of those whose names are not written in the Lamb's book of life.

First, we will deal with the controversy over the three words mentioned above. Then, we will look at how the Lord dealt with the subject Himself and how He instructed the Apostle John to write Hell's conclusion in the book of Revelation.

About 200 years before the birth of Christ, the Hebrew Scriptures were translated into the Greek language. This translation is known as the Septuagint. It can be clearly seen that the Hebrew word *sheol* was never translated into its Greek equivalent *hades,* for grave or burial place in the ground. *Sheol* was consistently translated into the Greek word *hades*, the place of departed spirits. Furthermore, in both Hebrew and Greek, there are two words for *grave*. One is the place of departed spirits; the other is the place where the body is laid at death. A good example of both Hebrew words is found in Genesis. *Sheol* is the place of departed spirits and *kever* is the burial place in an earthly grave.

> Genesis 37:35 —
> *And all his sons and all his daughters rose up to comfort him; but he refused to be comforted; and he said, For I will go down into the grave [07585 sheol] unto my son mourning. Thus his father wept for him.*

> Genesis 50:5 —
> *My father made me swear, saying, Lo, I die: in my grave [06913 kever] which I have digged for me in the land of Canaan, there shalt thou bury me. Now therefore let me go up, I pray thee, and bury my father, and I will come again.*

Dr. Robert A. Morey is the author of *Death and*

the Afterlife and over 40 other works, some of which have become classics. I stayed in his home in Pennsylvania during the 1990's. In his basement study he had over 10,000 volumes that he had read. He learned Hebrew at the age of 17 and is one of the leading apologists of our generation. During my various stays in his home, I learned much from him about the afterlife. Consider some of his comments on different words used for grave:

> *Not once is Hades the Greek equivalent of the Hebrew word for grave (kever). Not once does it mean nonexistence or unconsciousness. The times it is used for words other than Sheol it clearly means the world of spirits. There is, therefore, no way to escape the conclusion that the translators of the Septuagint clearly understood that Hades referred to the realm of disembodied souls or spirits; and, we must also emphasize, that the translators of the Septuagint did not obtain this concept from Platonic Greek thought but from the Hebrew concept of Sheol itself.*[42]

There are also two words for *grave* in the Greek. Morey points out that the word *hades* is a compound: the negative "not" and "seen," simply meaning *unseen*. He makes the point that graves where bodies are placed can be seen, but the souls in Hades cannot be seen. There are two different words for *grave*, with two different destinations.[43]

Besides *sheol*, *hades* and *gehenna*, there is a fourth word that is used in connection with Hell: *fire*. When fire is linked to Hell it describes a condition of torment. If Hell is the condition of unconsciousness or nonexistence, then why add *fire*, which creates the thought of being burned and the feeling of horrifying pain? The words "hell" and "fire," when they are used together, speak of two things: a place and a condition. They are thoroughly consistent with the Lord's teachings.

The Lord used the Greek word *gehenna*, which was the valley of Hinnom. It was a place where Israel offered their children as burnt sacrifices unto pagan gods. It was not just any place; it was a place of pain and torment. *Gehenna* does not, in any way, present the imagery of sleep or unconsciousness. Josiah desecrated the valley of Hinnom by making it into a city dump where the fires burned continuously to consume its waste (2 Kings 23:10).

When the Lord spoke of everlasting fire or hellfire and used *gehenna*, the people understood it to be a literal place of never-ending fire. There are twelve places in the New Testament where *gehenna* is used. Each time you see hell or hell fire in these verses, it is *gehenna*. Here are just a few examples where God warns people of His coming judgment upon the unsaved. They will spend eternity in Hell, which is described as a lake of fire.

> Matthew 5:22 –
> *But I say unto you, That whosoever is angry with his brother without a cause shall be in danger of the judgment: and whosoever shall say to his brother, Raca, shall be in danger of the council: but whosoever shall say, Thou fool, shall be in danger of hell fire.*

> Matthew 10:28 –
> *And fear not them which kill the body, but are not able to kill the soul: but rather fear him which is able to destroy both soul and body in hell* [a lake of fire].

In the light of this truth, consider the following observations: first, it is obvious that the soul is not the physical life of the body; otherwise, when the body would die, the soul would die. They are two separate parts. Killing the physical body would not kill the soul.

Second, the word "destroy" does not mean to perish into nonexistence. A building can be destroyed, yet it still exists in a different form. A person's life can be destroyed by alcohol or drugs, but he still exists in pain and misery.

Third, the Lord is giving man a strong warning regarding what man should fear. He said that one should fear hellfire, not physical death. Sodom and Gomorrah stand as an example to all: God will punish the wicked with fire. The inhabitants of these two cities felt the fiery brimstones fall from the heavens. Then, they found themselves in *sheol* where the conditions did not change. After the Great White Throne judgment, described in Revelation 20, they (and all those who are separated from God) will be cast into the lake of fire.

>Matthew 23:15 –
>*Woe unto you, scribes and Pharisees, hypocrites! for ye compass sea and land to make one proselyte, and when he is made, ye make him twofold more the child of hell than yourselves.*
>
>Matthew 23:33 –
>*Ye serpents, ye generation of vipers, how can ye escape the damnation of hell?*
>
>Luke 12:5 –
>*But I will forewarn you whom ye shall fear:*

> *Fear him, which after he hath killed hath power to cast into hell; yea, I say unto you, Fear him.*

Those who reject what the Bible teaches about eternal punishment should pay special attention to Mark 9:47. For, from the beginning of creation, the kingdom of God has always existed in two places: in heaven and on earth. The context, of Mark 9:47 and John 3, in no way limits the kingdom of God to a 144,000 people, as the JWs teach, nor does it divide hell into stages of glory like the Mormons teach.

In Mark 9:47, Jesus spoke about entering into the kingdom of God. When Jesus talked to Nicodemus (John 3:5), He told Nicodemus that, except a man be born-again (has a spiritual birth from God), he will not see or enter into the kingdom of God. Those who do not enter into the kingdom of God will enter into the lake of fire.

> Mark 9:43-48 –
> *And if thy hand offend thee, cut it off: it is better for thee to enter into life maimed, than having two hands to go into hell, into the fire that never shall be quenched:*
> *44 Where their worm dieth not, and the fire is not quenched.*
> *45 And if thy foot offend thee, cut it off: it is*

better for thee to enter halt into life, than having two feet to be cast into hell, into the fire that never shall be quenched:
46 Where their worm dieth not, and the fire is not quenched.
47 And if thine eye offend thee, pluck it out: it is better for thee to enter into the kingdom of God with one eye, than having two eyes to be cast into hell fire:
48 Where their worm dieth not, and the fire is not quenched.

If *hell* is a place of knowing nothing or a reference to the grave into which we go at death, then Jesus' statements about *hell* would make no sense. Jesus said that, if your hand, foot, or eye cause you to sin, it would be better to remove that hand, foot or eye, than to go into hell, "where their worm dieth not, and the fire is not quenched" (Mark 9:44).

To illustrate His point, Jesus gave an example of what happens to two people when they die, one who was saved and one who was lost.

Luke 16:19-24 –
There was a certain rich man, which was clothed in purple and fine linen, and fared sumptuously every day:
20 And there was a certain beggar named Lazarus, which was laid at his gate, full of

sores,
21 And desiring to be fed with the crumbs which fell from the rich man's table: moreover the dogs came and licked his sores.
22 And it came to pass, that the beggar died, and was carried by the angels into Abraham's bosom: the rich man also died, and was buried;
23 And in hell he lift up his eyes, being in torments, and seeth Abraham afar off, and Lazarus in his bosom.
24 And he cried and said, Father Abraham, have mercy on me, and send Lazarus, that he may dip the tip of his finger in water, and cool my tongue; for I am tormented in this flame.

When Jesus spoke of hell (Mark 9:43-48) and then illustrated its literal application (Luke 16:19-24), He made it possible for another "checkmate." There is no wiggle-room for JWs or anyone else who finds it fearful to accept the truth of an eternal punishment that is both physical and mental.

There is one final example that proves lost people will be in hell and in torment, without a second chance, forever. It is found in the Revelation. During the great tribulation, the Devil is served by two key men, literal men. One is the false prophet;

the other is the antichrist, who is also referred to as the beast. All three of them (the Devil, the false prophet and the antichrist) will be cast into the lake of fire; but, the question is, "When?" Look at the answer!

> Revelation 19:20 –
> *And the beast was taken, and with him the false prophet that wrought miracles before him, with which he deceived them that had received the mark of the beast, and them that worshipped his image. These both were cast alive into a lake of fire burning with brimstone.*

Both of those men, the false prophet and the antichrist, were cast alive into the lake of fire. Look carefully at the time: they are cast into the lake of fire at the beginning of the 1000 year reign of Christ. Now, near the end of the millennium, these same two men are seen again. Where are they seen? They are both seen, still alive, in the lake of fire after 1000 years (Revelation 20:10).

There is no second chance, no escaping and no hope. Like those men who are forever in the state of destruction without end, all who die without receiving the Jesus of the Bible will suffer forever. Then, the final enemy of God and of all His children, the Devil, will find himself in the place that was prepared especially for him, the lake of fire. Picture this scene in your mind.

> Revelation 20:10 –
> *And the devil that deceived them was cast into the lake of fire and brimstone, where the beast and the false prophet are* [two men who are still alive and will be tormented forever], *and shall be tormented day and night for ever and ever.*

There are two eternal places for men and angels. One is with God; the other is without God. There are also two eternal conditions. One is the state of eternal bliss for those who are with God; the other is the state of eternal torment for those who are not with God. Which eternality do you desire?

> John 6:47 –
> *Verily, verily, I say unto you, He that believeth on me hath everlasting life.*

Once you have believed upon the Lord Jesus Christ, you will do well to ask Him, "Lord, what would you have me to do?"

As He said, go ye:

> Matthew 28:18-20 –
> *All power is given unto me in heaven and in*

earth.

19 Go ye therefore, and teach all nations, baptizing them in the name of the Father, and of the Son, and of the Holy Ghost:

20 Teaching them to observe all things whatsoever I have commanded you: and, lo, I am with you alway, even unto the end of the world. Amen.

Endnotes

[1] *Gospel Principles,* (1997, Salt Lake City, LDS), p. 307, "Article 8."

[2] [Wikipedia.org/wiki/Robert_J._Matthews], Aug., 2013.

[3] Robert James Matthews, "A Plainer Translation: Joseph Smith's Translation of the Bible," (1985, Provo, Utah, ??), p.763 [http://eom.byu.edu/index.php/Joseph_Smith_Translation_of_the_Bible_(JST)].

[4] Ibid.

[5] Ibid.

[6] Brigham Young, 2nd President, *Journal of Discourses* (May 14, 1871, digital pub: BYU) 14:116.

[7] Ed Decker, *Decker's Complete Handbook on Mormonism*, (1995, Eugene, OR; Harvest House Publishers), p. 120.

[8] James Hattori, NBC correspondent, *Believer's flock to see statue 'weep' blood tears,"* (updated November 28, 2005, TODAY), Sacramento, California, 10:12:25 AM ET.

[9] [Mormonwiki.org/Burning_in_the_bosom].

[10] Doctrines and Covenants, Section 9, verse 8, [www.lds.org/scriptures/dc-testament].

Endnotes *(continued)*

[11] Cary McMullen, "Holding Their Tongues," [*Christianity Today, Holding Their Tongues, Cary McMullen in Orlando [9/21/2009 9:45:56 AM]*.

[12] *What Does the Bible Really Teach?*, (2005, Brooklyn, Watch Tower Bible and Tract Society of Pennsylvania), p. 41.

[13] *Doctrine and Covenants,* 93:21.

[14] *Discourses of Brigham Young, p. 26* [*Gospel Principles,* 1997, p. 11].

[15] J. Mark Martin (compiler), *Seventh Day Adventism and the Writings of Ellen G. White,* citing: E.G. White, *Spiritual Gifts*, vol. 2, p. 276. http://www.bereanpublishers.com/seventh_day_adventism_and_the_writings_of_ellen_g_white/#Part%202:%2014%20_%2038].

[16] *Watchtower,* 1995, p. 20.

[17] *Watchtower,* 1950, p. 236.

[18] *Watchtower,* April 1st, 2009, p. 7.

[19] *Watchtower,* 1958, p. 559.

[20] *Watchtower*, 1953, p. 518.

[21] *Watchtower,* 1979, p. 31.

Endnotes *(continued)*

[22] *Watchtower,* 1991, p. 28.

[23] *Watchtower,* 1974, p. 478.

[24] *You Can Live Forever in Paradise on Earth,* 1989, p.195, par. 13-14.

[25] *Watchtower,* 2004, p. 12, par. 18.

[26] Watchtower's October 6, 2012, *128th Annual Meeting Report,* Jersey City, NJ [http://www.jw.org/en/news/events-activities/annual-meeting-report-2012/].

[27] *Doctrine and Covenants,* 131:1-4 (*Decker's Complete Handbook on Mormonism,* p. 128).

[28] *Gospel Principles,* 1997, p. 303.

[29] Ibid., p. 305.

[30] Ibid., p. 307, "Article 8."

[31] *Watchtower,* 1950, p. 516, par. 2.

[32] *Watchtower, Your Will Be Done on Earth* (January 15, 1959), part 6, p. 58, par. 32-33.

[33] *What Does The Bible Really Teach?* (2009, Brooklyn, Watch Tower Bible and Tract Society of Pennsylvania), p. 214-215.

Endnotes (*continued*)

[34] Lewis Sperry Chafer, *Systematic Theology* (1971, Dallas, Dallas Seminary Press) vol. 2, p. 7.

[35] Lewis Sperry Chafer, *Major Bible Themes* (*Revised Edition*, by John F. Walvoord (1974, Grand Rapids, Zondervan), p. 373.

[36] Randy Alcorn, *Heaven,* (2004, Carol Stream, IL, Tyndale Publishers, Inc.), p. 211.

[37] *Gospel Principles,* p. 379.

[38] Ibid.

[39] Ibid.

[40] M. James Penton, *Apocalypse Delayed: The Story of Jehovah's Witnesses,* (1997, Toronto, University of Toronto Press), p.15.

[41] *You Can Live Forever in Paradise on Earth*, (Watchtower Books), chapter 9, p.88, par. 19-20.

[42] Robert A. Morey, *Death and the Afterlife*, (1984, Minneapolis, Bethany House Publishers), p.82.

[43] Morey, p. 25.

Bibliography

Alcorn, Randy. *Heaven*. Carol Stream, IL. Tyndale. 2004.

Chafer, Lewis Sperry. *Systematic Theology*. Dallas. Dallas Seminary Press. 1971.

_____. Revised by John F. Walvoord. *Major Bible Themes:Revised Edition*. Grand Rapids. Zondervan. 1974.

Decker, Ed. *Decker's Complete Handbook on Mormonism*. Eugene, OR. Harvest House Publishers. 1995.

Doctrines and Covenants. LDS.

Gospel Principles. Salt Lake City. LDS. 1997.

Hattori, James (NBC Correspondent). *Believers flock to see statue 'weep' blood tears*. Nov. 28, 2005. [www.TODAY.com]. Sacramento, California.

Martin, J. Mark (compiler), *Seventh Day Adventism and the Writings of Ellen G. White*, citing: E.G. White, *Spiritual Gifts*, vol. 2, p. 276. [http://www.bereanpublishers.com/seventh_day_adventism_and_the_writings_of_ellen_g_white/#Part%202:%2014%20_%2038].

Matthews, Robert James. *A Plainer Translation: Joseph Smith's Translation of the Bible*. Provo, Utah. 1985.

Bibliography (*continued*)

McMullen, Cary. *Holding Their Tongues. Christianity Today.* 21 September 2009. [*Christianity Today, Holding Their Tongues, Cary McMullen in Orlando 9/21/2009 9:45:56 AM*].

Morey, Robert A. *Death and the Afterlife.* Minneapolis. Bethany House Publishers. 1984.

Mormonwiki.org/Burning_in_the_bosom.

Penton, M. James. *Apocalypse Delayed: The Story of Jehovah's Witnesses.* Toronto. University of Toronto Press. 1997.

Thomas, Catherine M. *What do Mormons Believe about Hell. Encyclopedia of Mormonism.* BYU. 28 March 2008. [http://www.whatdomormons believe.com/2009/04/what-do-mormons-believe-about-hell/].

What does the Bible Really Teach? Brooklyn. New York. Watch Tower Bible and Tract Society of Pennsylvania. 2005.

Watchtower, Watch Tower Bible and Tract Society of Pennsylvania. 1950. 1953. 1958. 1959. 1974. 1979. 1991. 1995. 2004. 2009.

Watchtower and Tract Society of Pennsylvania. 128th *Annual Meeting Report.* Jersey City, New Jersey. 2012.

Bibliography (*continued*)

Wikipedia.org/wiki/Robert_J._Matthews. 2013.

Young, Brigham. *Journal of Discourses*. BYU. 1871.

You Can Live Forever in Paradise on Earth. Brooklyn. Watchtower Books. 1989.

Scripture Index

Acts

5:12 — 22

Colossians

1:15 — 89, 90
1:15-16 — 39
1:15-18 — 86, 89, 90
1:16 — 85, 90
1:18 — 91

1 Corinthians

11:3 — 83
15:20 — 91

2 Corinthians

5:8 — 108
11:13-15 — 25
12:2-4 — 106
12:12 — 22

Daniel

7:1, 13-14 — 44
10:13 — 62-64, 66
10:21 — 63
12:1 — 63

Genesis

1:1 — 47, 51, 84
1:14 — 107
1:2 — 84
1:20 — 109
1:26 — 47, 51
1:27 — 85
3:1-4 — 7
3:1c — 100
3:4b — 100
3:21 — 5
4:1 — 87
37:35 — 125
41:50-52 — 88

50:5 — 125

Hebrews

7:3 — 38

Isaiah

65:17 — 113

James

1:5 — 23
2:14-26 — 14
2:21-23 — 54

Jeremiah

31:9 — 88

John

1:1 — 29-34, 79
1:1-3 — 36, 39, 48, 58, 78, 85
1:1-14 — 29-31
1:1a — 34, 38, 78
1:1b — 34
1:1c — 34
1:3 — 12, 13, 39-40, 84, 101
1:12 — 48
1:12-13 — 57
2:16 — 110-111
3:3 — 51
3:3-7 — 52, 56
3:5 — 130
3:7 — 43
6:47 — 134
10:28 — 4
14:2 — 110, 111
17:3 — 75-78
17:24 — 107, 117
18:36 — 113
19:34 — 80

1 John

2:4 — 55
2:29 — 59
3:9-10 — 58
4:14 — 76
5:20 — 77

Jude

1:9 — 62
1:25 — 76

1 Kings

8:30 — 106

2 Kings

23:10 — 127

Luke

8:15 — 99
12:5 — 129
16:19-24 — 130

Mark

9:43-48 — 130, 132
9:44 — 131
9:47 — 130

Matthew

4:1-10 — 8
4:10 — 65
5:18 — 14
5:22 — 128
10:28 — 128
12:40 — 21
16:1 — 20
16:4 — 21
18:10 — 106
21:43 — 47
23:15 — 129
23:33 — 129

Scripture Index

24 — 42
24:1 — 71
24:13 — 53
24:29 — 72
24:30 — 21
24:35 — 14, 17
24:44 — 72
24:44-51 — 70
24:47 — 71
26:63-64 — 44
28:18-20 — 134
28:19 — 77

2 Peter

3:10 — 112
3:13 — 112

Philippians

1:23 — 108
2:10-11 — 65

Proverbs

3:6 — 73
8:1-3 — 92
8:22 — 91

Psalm

11:4 — 106
37 — 52
37:11 — 113
37:29 — 51
89:27 — 39, 89
110:1 — 81
132:13-14 — 114

Revelation

1:7 — 22
1:19 — 68-69
3:14 — 91
4:1 — 68-69
5:3 — 109
6-18 — 70

7&14 — 41, 43, 72
7:13-15 — 109
12:7 — 64
13:11-15 — 26
16:14 — 26
17:14 — 64
19 — 72
19:20 — 133
20 — 129
20:10 — 133
21 — 95
21:1-4 — 113-114
21:9-10 — 115
21:27 — 115

Romans

4:1-5 — 53-54
10:17 — 98

1 Samuel

16:6 — 89

2 Samuel

16:11 — 89

1 Thessalonians

3:13 — 108
4:13-18 — 72
4:16 — 65
4:16-17 — 108

2 Thessalonians

2:9-12 — 25

2 Timothy

2:24-26 — 74

Zechariah

12:10 — 78, 79
14:3-4 — 78

Subject Index

1919 — 41, 70, 102
144,000 — 41-44, 50, 56, 67-68, 70, 72, 130

Abraham, 53-55, 122-123, 132
Adam, 5, 37, 50, 85, 87
Adventist "Jesus," 37
Annihilationism, 120, 122
Antichrist, 133
Apostle Paul: third heaven, 107
Archangels: more than one, 66
Armageddon, 70, 72, 80, 101, 104
Assemblies of God: speaking in tongues, 24
Authority: delegated, 46; headship, 84; of men, 31,121; of Scripture, 2, 7, 17, 27, 31, 100, 106
Bearing their testimony: Mormons, 15
Book of Mormon: superior to the Bible, 7, 99; read and pray, 15, 19, 23
Born-again: "checkmate," 43; definition, 48; no exceptions, 130
Burning of the bosom, 19
Cain, 87
Calvary: salvation, 5; who was pierced at Calvary, 80
Checkmate, 42
Children of God: must be born, 48, 49
Children of the Devil: the unrighteous, not born of God; 49, 52-53, 59
Christ: Creator of all things, 12, 36, 39, 49, 58, 99-100
Christ: His divinity, 78-82
Christ: His eternality, 34, 38, 79
Church age, 23, 67
Common grave, 120
Concepts, 33-34, 36
Conditionalism, 120
Conflicts, 1, 98
Context Rule, 4, 31
Conviction, 2, 19, 40

David: God's firstborn, 39, 80-81, 88; called Jehovah both LORD and Lord, 80-82
Decker, Ed, 94
Disfellowshipped, 121
Disfellowshipping, 62
Divinity: of Christ, 78-82
Eliab, 89
Elohim, 37
Ephraim, 87-89
Eschatology, 93, 117
Eternal punishment, 130, 132
Eve, 5, 85, 87
Ex-JW, 98, 121
Ex-Mormon, 94, 98
Facing the Facts, 61
Faith, 2, 14-15, 17, 19, 58
Faithful and Discrete Slave, 70
False Jesus, 15, 17, 36, 40, 42, 49, 55, 100
False prophet, 106, 133-134
Father's house, 110-112
Fire, 26, 74, 94, 111-112, 118-119, 127-131, 133-134
First created, 36, 48, 81, 85-86
First heaven, 107, 114
First Spirit Child, 37
Firstborn, 36, 39, 85-91
Gehenna, 124, 127-128
Goats, 52
god, 40, 48, 55, 96, 100
God the Father, 65, 83-84
God the Son, 76-77, 83-84
Godhead, 77, 83-84
gods, 77, 96, 127
Gomorrah, 129
Grace, 5, 42, 53, 80
Grave, 120, 122-123, 125-127, 131
Great Tribulation, 70-72, 109, 133
Grew, Henry, 121-122
Hades, 122-127
Harmony Rule, 4, 5
Hattori, James, 23
Heaven, 14, 17, 20-21, 26, 37, 39, 43, 45-51, 64-67, 69, 72, 84-86,

Subject Index

93-98, 100-103, 105-115, 117, 123, 129-130
Hell, 94, 109, 117-120, 122-124, 127-133
Hellfire, 119, 127, 129
Hinnom, valley of, 127
Holy Spirit, 23-24, 29, 34, 68, 73, 77, 83-85, 102
Hope, 3, 40, 42, 50, 56, 58, 73, 102-103, 134
Humanity (of Christ), 82
Immortality, 41, 96
Israel, 41, 60, 89, 106, 127
Jehovah, 36, 39, 62, 78-81, 101-104, 120-121
Jehovah is Jesus, 78, 80
Jehovah's Witnesses, 1, 41, 120-121
Jesse, 88-89
Jesus, 4, 12-13, 17, 21, 30-40, 42-45, 48-49, 57, 62, 65-66, 75-78, 81, 83-87, 89-92, 100, 108-113, 124, 130-134
Justified, 53-55
JW, 41
Kever, 125-126
Kingdom, 41, 43-51, 93-96, 101-102, 111-113, 115, 130-131
Kingdoms, two, 50-51
Kingdom of righteousness, 93-94
Lake of fire, 94, 124, 128-130, 133-134
Lamb's book of life, 105, 111, 113, 116, 124
Last Stand, 43, 75
Lazarus, 122-123, 132
Lost, 3, 27, 40, 42, 73- 74, 93, 99, 104, 131, 133
Lucifer, 50
Mary, 19, 23
Matthews, Robert J., 9
Matter, the creation of, 13
Meek, 113
Michael, 37, 75, 81
Millennial kingdom, 101
Morey, Robert A., 125

Mormonism, 16, 23, 137
Mormon Church, 11, 94
Mormon "Jesus," 12, 37, 40
Moslem "Jesus," 37
New Earth, 110-114
New Jerusalem, 105, 110-114
Nicodemus, 130
Objective truth, 20
Pentecostal, 16, 19, 24
Penton, M. James, 121
Pharisees, 129
Preeminence (of Christ), 86-87, 90
Redeemed, 105, 107-109, 112
Repentance, 5, 74
Resurrection, 21, 42, 59, 61-62, 91, 103, 118, 120
Righteous, 49-50, 52-56, 58-59, 93-94, 97, 105, 111-113, 115
Russell, Charles Taze, 61, 121
Sadducees, 20
Samuel, 89
Satan, 7-9, 17, 20, 23, 25, 27, 65, 105, 118, 120
Saved, 5-6, 25, 49-50, 131
Saviour, 27, 59, 76, 110, 117
Scriptures, 1, 2, 22, 32, 50, 54, 58, 124
Second chance, 104, 133-134
Second coming, 21
Second Heaven, 107
Septuagint, 125-126
Seventh-Day Adventists, 37, 61
Sheep, 49, 52, 89, 111
Sheol, 60, 124-127, 129
Sign (no sign given), 21
Signs of Satan, 17, 20, 22
Signs of the apostles, 17, 20, 23
Smith, Joseph, 97
Sodom, 129
Soul-sleep, 120
Spirit brother, 37
Spirit children, 96-97
Spirit of God, 3, 73, 84
Spirit-prison, 120
Spiritual birth, 130

Subject Index

Supernatural experience, 19
Tares (only two groups of people; tares and wheat), 49, 52
The beginning (Christ's eternality), 38
Third Heaven, 105, 107
Tongues, 16, 19,-20, 24
Tribulation, 70-72, 109, 133
Trinity, 41, 75-76, 83, 85
Triune, 75, 78, 83
Trump of God, 65-66, 69, 108
Truth, 98-100, 106, 128, 132
Virgin Mary, 23
Watchtower, 41, 46, 49-51, 56, 59, 61-62, 64-67, 70-72, 81, 101, 104, 120-122
Watchtower "Jesus," 36
Weapon, ultimate, 75
Wheat (only two groups of people; wheat and tares), 49, 52
Wicked, 21, 49, 52, 92, 118-119, 129
Wisdom, 92, 96, 115
Witness, 1, 42, 91, 94
Word of God, 98, 124
Works, 7, 14-15, 25, 53-55, 100, 103, 112